A CHEF AT YOUR ELBOW
RECIPES AND WRINKLES

Ian Lye

THE GALLEY

Published by:
Galley Publishing,
12 High Street, Watlington, Oxfordshire OX9 5PY

© 1999 Ian Lye

ISBN 0 9535569 0 5

Photography by Julia Hanson-Abbott

British Library Cataloguing in Publication Data:
a catalogue record for this book is available from the British Library.

Printed and bound by:
MFP Design & Print
Longford Trading Estate, Thomas Street, Stretford, Manchester M32 0JT

CONTENTS

—ooOoo—

4. INTRODUCTION

—ooOoo—

INTRODUCTION

The aim of A CHEF AT YOUR ELBOW is simply to help everyone who wants to be a better cook. Condensed into this one volume, you will find detailed instructions to enable you to master the cooking skills which will give good results every time, even for beginners.

My own interest in food and its preparation started at an early age, for I remember recipes and methods used by my mother, but it was not until I met my late French wife Jacqueline, who lived in Paris with her widowed mother and Aunt, that I started to cook seriously. 'Auntie' was my source of inspiration, she was a perfectionist and, although she spoke no English and I no French, such was our mutual love of food that she was happy to teach me. She also taught Jacqui, who in turn instructed me, so that is where it all began! You will find a number of references to 'Auntie' throughout my book.

During a long career as a restaurateur and caterer I have been asked umpteen times, by even some very experienced cooks, for the secrets of pastry making, sauces, fish cooking, omelettes, green vegetables etc., which they have been unable to find adequately answered in their recipe books.

Allow me to tell you about professional methods and techniques and then let me talk you through some of my favourite recipes and you will have at your fingertips a small, varied repertoire to act as a springboard to further success.

There is today a growing nostalgia for good 'old-fashioned' food, without complicated or difficult-to-obtain ingredients and conflicting tastes. All my recipes come directly from the simplicity of traditional French and English cooking and demonstrate that French food need not be rich, nor English food stodgy. Many customers, family and friends for whom I have enjoyed cooking over the years have called these dishes REAL food.

At the same time, there is a growing awareness of the importance of healthy eating and of the merits of the 'Mediterranean Diet' which contains plenty of fresh vegetables and olive oil. I have, over the years, modified many of my recipes and now use as much olive oil, in place of butter, as I can. It is, however, absolutely essential to use only a high grade oil, to avoid tainting a dish with olive oil flavour. I find French or Italian first cold pressed oil, although expensive, gives a perfect result. You will find in many recipes that I also use potato flour, instead of wheat flour, which is not only easier to use, but more easily digestible.

It is often the preparation, as much as the cooking, that gives good results and good quality, fresh ingredients are essential. My old grandmother used to say "You cannot make a silk purse out of a sow's ear!"

Finally, keep it simple. The most memorable meals are the least pretentious.

Cooking is fun — I hope you will enjoy it as much as I do.

KITCHEN EQUIPMENT

choosing and looking after basic kitchen equipment

KITCHEN EQUIPMENT

When choosing the equipment for your kitchen you should bear in mind the maximum number of people you will have to cook for. You can always cook less in a large pan. The more versatile your equipment, the more use you will get from it.

Always buy the best you can afford. There is a wide range of pots and pans, utensils and gadgets on the market, but cooking is easier with heavyweight, professional tools and they will give years of service. Lightweight pans will never give as good a result, particularly for sauce making, as a heavyweight pan with a good thick base. A thin pan will have uneven heat distribution or 'hot spots' which cause sticking and therefore scorching and burning.

My own kitchen equipment is very simple, based on my favourite Chasseur cast-iron, copper and good knives.

CAST IRON

The only criticism I have heard repeatedly is the heavy weight of cast iron, but, for the serious cook, all top grade professional pans, be they stainless steel, copper or cast iron, are heavy. The advantages are of good , even heat distribution, stability, and therefore safety. So you will find throughout this book that I recommend Chasseur products, which answer all the requirements of a good pan.

Chasseur is well established in the cast iron market. Made in a range of attractive colours to co-ordinate with kitchen and dining room, it also matches the Aga colours and is suitable for all heat sources including induction. It can be used on top of the stove or in the oven and is good looking enough to serve from at table, keeping food hot during a leisurely and enjoyable meal. Aways lift rather than drag across a ceramic hob to avoid damage.

Use wooden or nylon utensils in enamelled cast iron, as metal utensils may mark and, over time, damage the surface. Easy to clean, it is only necessary to soak to remove even burnt on food.

STAINLESS STEEL

Saucepans and frying pans, when made with a thick aluminium or copper sandwich base, are robust, good looking and easy to care for. They are excellent general purpose pans. The thick base gives good, even heat distribution. Stainless steel stockpots are good to use on top of the stove for large quantities.

Stainless steel pans may sometimes stick in use, particularly if you are making a roux or using flour. The solution is to remove the pan from the heat for a minute or two and the food will release.

Stainless steel roasting pans are also excellent. Choose one that is not too deep, as this will allow the hot air to circulate better round the roasting joint.

Recently developed and now available are multi-layered stainless steel pans. Instead of the traditional sandwich base, these pans are made throughout of super conductive materials. One such range is Cristal from Spring of Switzerland. This type of pan costs more, but they have many of the advantages previously only available in professional copper pans.

When using stainless steel pans, **never put salt in the water until it is boiling**. If put into cold water, salt will leave white spots on the surface of the pan. Sometimes the natural salt in foods will leave these same spots. Clean with a nylon scouring pad and nonscratch cleaner. If you should have a badly burnt pan and soaking doesn't do the trick, boil up some biological washing powder in the pan, then leave it to soak again. Even really badly burnt pans can be resurrected in this way. Use stainless steel cleaner to keep the pans sparkling.

CARBON STEEL

Used extensively in commercial kitchens, carbon steel frying pans are inexpensive and suitable for use over high heats for frying or 'sealing' meats. Choose a heavy gauge, as these will not distort and are suitable for all types of stove. Although not glamorous, becoming blackened with use, they are virtually indestructible. But not for those who want an easy-care pan.

A new carbon steel pan needs to be 'seasoned' before use. To do this, sprinkle the pan generously with salt and put on a high heat, shaking it until the salt has turned brown. When the pan has cooled take a ball of kitchen paper and scour the pan thoroughly with the salt, then wipe it clean and finish with a film of cooking oil. The pan is now ready to use. After washing, always thoroughly dry the pan and then wipe it round with kitchen paper and a small amount of oil to prevent rusting.

NON-STICK

Many inexpensive non-stick coatings have a limited life if high heats are used, but good, modern non-stick surfaces are especially designed to withstand high heats. For pancake making a non-stick pan is suitable and very easy to use. Choose a pan with a thick base like the Hackman Panny range from Finland, which I have found ideal.

Only use nylon or wooden utensils, metal will damage the surface.

ANODISED ALUMINIUM

The process of anodising produces a surface harder than steel and eliminates the health objections to the use of aluminium. A good, all over even heat distribution makes these pans practical for all uses, but they are not dishwasher safe.

COPPER

Copper lined with stainless steel, is the choice of many professional chefs. Always buy the heavy, professional gauge, anything less will work out more costly in the end, as it will not give the lifetime of service you can expect from the best.

Before stainless steel was used to line copper pans, they were lined with tin, which became worn with use and needed expensive retinning. It is well worth paying the extra for stainless steel lining.

Copper is perfect for omelette making and I keep a pan especially for omelettes, but I wash it as little as possible! To clean, simply heat it up and then give it a really good rub round with salt and kitchen paper.

You can now get excellent paste copper cleaners which are washed off under hot water — no more black hands and dusters and polishing! After cleaning, and before using the omelette pan again, give the inside a good rousting with dry kitchen paper and finish with a film of cooking oil. If the pan sticks, use dry salt with the paper.

KNIVES

This is a whole subject in itself! The original carbon steel has now been almost entirely replaced by those made from stainless steel.

Excellent knives are those which are fully forged with the blade, bolster and tang made from one piece of steel, giving strength and security. The handle can either be moulded or riveted. These knives are strong and well balanced

There are also some very good taper-ground knives without any bolster, which are nonetheless good, but beware of inexpensive knives with whippy blades, these will bend and slip when in use and can cost you the odd cut finger!

J.A. Henckels have always been the benchmark for quality knives. They are the choice of many professional cooks and use a unique advanced technology whereby differing grades of steel are combined to form a single integral piece so that the blade, bolster and tang have the best characteristics for the job. A good knife will make all your kitchen work quicker, safer and easier.

Knives should be stored in a knife block or rack, not loose in a drawer, where the blades will get damaged. Avoid, as much as possible, putting them in the dishwasher, as the chemicals in some washing-up powders can damage the blades.

Knives should be sharpened a little and often. A couple of strokes on the sharpener every time you use them is best. The sharper the knife, not only the easier to use, but also the safer, as it will not slip or tear. To sharpen with a steel, hold the knife at quite an acute angle to the steel, about 20%, and draw the blade down towards the handle of the steel in an arc from base to tip. If you are not adept with a steel, use a good quality sharpener sparingly.

PORCELAIN

Being fired at very high temperatures, porcelain can withstand high heats in the oven or under the grill. You will find oven-to-table ware in porcelain excellent for gratins, baking and pâté making. Having a hard, non-porous surface, porcelain is very easy to clean, even burnt on food only needs a soak. Chasseur make an attractive range to match their cast iron.

EARTHENWARE

Earthenware is also good for paté making and casseroling. It absorbs and retains heat well, giving a good, all round heat during cooking.

But, being fired at a lower temperature to porcelain is more prone to chipping and crazing.

UTENSILS

I use stainless steel utensils, as these are hard wearing and do not rust.

When it comes to larger equipment, a food

processor makes light work of so many tasks that it will earn its keep over and over again, as will a good mixer. I also use a good old-fashioned mincer, although mincer attachments are also made for electric mixers.

WOODEN UTENSILS

A good chopping board is an essential. Some years ago the health and hygiene gurus, in their wisdom, advocated that chopping boards should be made of plastic, as these were considered to be more hygienic than wood. A number of years later research found that, in fact, wood contains natural properties which inhibit the growth and spread of bacteria! So I advocate a wooden chopping board. In fact, you will find it helpful to have more than one. To avoid cross-contamination of foods, wash your board thoroughly after preparing raw meat or fish and before using it for vegetables, salads or fruit.

I also prefer wooden spoons to plastic!

TINWARE

For baking you will need a selection of suitable tins. Removable base tins are useful for quiches, tarts and cakes. You can go for the traditional heavy tinware, or there are now a number of tins with a quick release anodised or non-stick finish that make baking easy. The heavier the tin, the better it will bake and retain its shape.

—ooOoo—

THE STORE CUPBOARD

keeping a useful store cupboard &
advance preparation for economy and speed

THE STORE CUPBOARD

I thought it might be useful to give a little guidance on stocking a store cupboard. The contents of such a larder will obviously vary, but to tackle the repertoire in this book you would require a stock similar to mine and the following list is my kitchen 'come-in-handy-locker.'

DRY GOODS

Sea Salt	Plain Flour	Gelatine	Basmati Rice
Black Peppercorns	Self-Raising Flour	French Mustard	Pasta
Whole Pickling Spice	Potato Flour	Tomato Purée	Yellow Split Peas
Whole Nutmeg	Groundnut Oil	Chicken Stock Cubes	Granulated Sugar
Dried Thyme	Olive Oil	Vanilla Essence	Caster Sugar
Dried Sage	(1st Cold Pressing)	Sultanas	Coffee
Dried Tarragon	Red Wine Vinegar	Raisins & Currants	Tea
Bay Leaves	White Wine Vinegar		

Sea salt is the healthiest way of taking in the salt we need for health and seasoning. Freshly ground black pepper retains the oils that give it its distinctive full aroma. Spices were used in traditional English cooking and I use pickling spice in several of my recipes. They will not deteriorate with keeping; spices buried in Egyptian tombs were found thousands of years later to be in perfect condition. Dried herbs, however, will deteriorate over time and are best kept away from light and heat. You will find that in my recipes I keep the herbs very simple and use mostly dried thyme and fresh parsley, which is easy to obtain and can be kept in the fridge. This is in recognition of the busy lives we all lead nowadays and, because fresh herbs do not last long, they can be wasteful.

However, where possible, you may well like to substitute fresh herbs in some recipes and experiment with others.

I use potato flour for thickening many sauces and soups. It is lighter than ordinary flour and very easy to use. It is available from health food shops and supermarkets.

What oil you use will be very much a matter of taste. I like to use a mild olive oil. Many are very strong and pungent and I find first, cold-pressed virgin olive oil, mostly from Italy or France, the best, and mild enough not to overpower in cooking. Spanish olive oils are usually stronger in flavour. I also use groundnut oil, another pleasantly mild oil, either on its own or combined with olive oil. I now avoid vegetable oils, since it is often not clear what 'vegetable' oils they contain and I am not happy with any genetically altered plants until we know more about their effect.

TINNED GOODS

Salmon	Tuna in Oil	Sardines	Tomatoes
Sweet Gherkins	Black Olives	Anchovy Fillets	Peas (French)

French tinned peas, which can now be found in most supermarkets are a great standby and are quite different to English peas. They are delicious with fish and grills. To use, heat up the peas, then thicken the sauce with a little potato flour mixed with cold water and add $\frac{1}{2}$ teaspoon of caster sugar, freshly ground black pepper and a small knob of butter. The sauce is an integral part of the dish.

IN THE FRIDGE

Parmesan Cheese	Gruyere or	Block Margarine	Lard
Unsalted Butter	Cheddar Cheese	Eggs	Milk

Unsalted butter is better for cooking than salted, as the salt (as well as the milk content, see clarified butter p.26) burns easily. I keep block margarine and lard for pastry making.

IN THE DEEP FREEZE

Stock	Basic Brown Sauce	Bread	Cooked Spinach
Fish Stock	Sauce Provençale		

By having some stock and basic sauces in your freezer you will be able to make many sauces and dishes at short notice and with a minimum of preparation time (see Quick Stocks & Sauce Making p.13).

Time can also be saved by making larger quantities of soup and casseroles and putting some away in the freezer for later use.

QUICK STOCKS, DRESSINGS & SAUCE MAKING

introduction to techniques, preparation,
making in advance and recipes

STOCKS & SAUCES

Stocks made from bones or carcasses form the basis of many soups and sauces, adding that extra flavour so important to the result. But beware! never use lamb gravy or stock in any recipe apart from lamb dishes, as its distinctive flavour cannot be masked.

If insufficient fresh stock is available, I substitute chicken cubes, but sparingly! I only ever use **chicken** stock cubes, even in fish sauces, as I find beef and fish cubes too overpowering.

Most commercial kitchens have a stockpot simmering on the stove for hours and this is in daily use. The domestic kitchen has neither the demand nor the facilities to run a stockpot. However, whenever you have chicken or meat bones, do not throw them away, but make a simple stock from them. You can then divide the stock into suitable containers and put it into the deep-freeze ready to use later.

This chapter starts with a few words of guidance for making these quick stocks. To add extra flavour to any of these, include a little onion, carrot, tomato ends, mushroom peelings and a bay leaf. You will notice that I tell you to boil stock without a lid. **Stock made with a lid on, or boiled too fast, will be cloudy**. Some sauce dishes in this book are complete in themselves and the recipes for these contain full instructions. This chapter deals with an assortment of sauces, hot and cold, which have a more general application.

When making sauces, **a good saucepan is essential**. Chasseur with its all-round heat diffusion is ideal.

Some cooks recommend using a whisk for sauce making, but I disagree. Whisks tend to get clogged and a wooden spoon will better reach the edges of the saucepan, making the whole process easier.

If you can master the making of a béchamel sauce, you will be able to make any flour-based sauce and a little practice is well worthwhile. It is important, for the perfect result, to blend the butter and flour into a 'roux' and **cook this well** before adding any liquid, which should be hot, otherwise your sauce will be gluey or floury. **Add only a little liquid at a time** and, if your sauce is threatening to become lumpy, remove the pan from the heat and stir vigorously until the liquid has been smoothly absorbed, then return the pan to the heat again.

Don't be gentle, knock the sauce about briskly with the spoon!

Also included are instructions for making clarified butter, and an easy way to make a sachet for Bouquet Garni, spices or cloves.

—ooOoo—

CHICKEN STOCK

Simply simmer raw or cooked chicken carcasses, giblets and trimmings in water for one hour, **without a lid**, and strain. **Don't boil too long**, for this will produce a bitter flavour.

—ooOoo—

LAMB STOCK

Lamb stock should **only** be used in lamb dishes, as its distinctive flavour cannot be masked. Simmer bones and trimmings, either raw or cooked for approximately $1\frac{1}{2}$ to 2 hours, **without a lid**, to produce a nice, clear stock, then strain.

—ooOoo—

BEEF STOCK

Ask your butcher for marrow bones and get him to split them for you. Two large marrow bones will make about two pints of stock.

Place them in a roasting dish, paint with oil, and place in a **preheated** oven 220°C/Gas Mark 7 for one hour.

Transfer to a large pot, cover with water and simmer for approximately 2 hours, **without a lid**. Do not boil fast! Check the liquid from time to time and top up as required. Strain to use.

—ooOoo—

VEAL STOCK

If you can find veal marrow bones, they produce wonderful stock. The method is the same as for beef stock.

FISH STOCK

This is made from raw fish bones and the white skin **— do not use the black skin as this will discolour your stock.** Also, **only use plaice bones if you are making a plaice dish,** as these have a strongly distinctive flavour and will spoil other dishes.

Put the bones and skins into a saucepan, well covered with water and simmer for 30 minutes — **not more**! Keep the water topped up, if necessary, so that you finish with enough stock to just cover the bones etc. Strain to use.

If you have no fish stock when this is required for a dish you can, perhaps surprisingly, use a little chicken stock cube (**fish cubes are too over-powering**).

—ooOoo—

15

BASIC BROWN SAUCE

This sauce is the base used for several sauces including Madeira Sauce p.127 and Piquant Sauce p.128.

IT CAN BE MADE IN ADVANCE, divided and kept in suitably sized containers in the freezer ready for use.

TO MAKE 1 LITRE /1³/₄ PINTS. YOU WILL NEED:

2 Carrots
1 Large Onion
1 Stick of Celery
1 Clove of Garlic
2 Tablespoons of Tomato Purée
1200ml /2 pints Chicken or Meat Stock (see p.15)
90gr /3oz Plain Flour
90gr /3oz Unsalted Butter
Sprig of Parsley
Sprig of Thyme /or ¹/₂ tsp dried
1 Bay Leaf
150ml/¹/₄ pint Red Wine
Salt and Freshly Milled Black Pepper

METHOD
1. Peel and roughly chop the vegetables.
2. Peel, cut and crush the garlic.
3. Heat the stock in a saucepan and set on one side.
4. Melt the butter in a thick based saucepan over a medium heat, add the vegetables, garlic and herbs and cook for 3 minutes, stirring from time to time.
5. Add the tomato purée and stir, then add the flour, stirring vigorously to form a roux and continue to cook for 1 – 2 minutes.
6. Remove your pan from the heat for a moment and add a little hot stock, put back on the heat and, stirring all the time to prevent lumps, gradually add the rest of the stock and then the red wine, until you have a slightly thin sauce texture.
7. Turn the heat down to simmer for 20 minutes, stirring from time to time to stop the sauce from sticking to the saucepan and burning.
8. Pass the sauce through a fine sieve, **using a pastry brush** to speed the liquid through. **Don't use a spoon** or you will push unwanted bits of vegetables and herbs through and spoil the texture of your sauce.

Check for seasoning but **do not over season** or you may get too salty a result when you make your final sauce.

—ooOoo—

BÉCHAMEL SAUCE

This classic French sauce is the one which every aspiring chef must master. In professional kitchens it is often used as a test of aptitude and ability. It is also the basis for cheese (mornay) sauce, which follows, and see also white sauce to serve with vegetables. With practice you will make béchamel sauce without exact measurements, being guided by the consistency.

TO MAKE APPROX. 600ML /1 PINT YOU WILL NEED

60gr /2oz Unsalted Butter
60gr /2oz Plain Flour
600ml /1 pint Milk
A Little Cream (optional)
A Pinch of Salt

METHOD

1. Heat the milk.
2. Melt the butter in another saucepan and blend in the flour and salt, **stirring vigorously** with a wooden spoon.
3. Cook over a medium heat for 1 to 2 minutes, stirring continuously, but **do not brown**! It is important to **thoroughly cook your roux** or your sauce will be gluey or floury. At this stage the roux should have the consistency of fatty breadcrumbs.

This next stage needs caution for, if you add too much liquid at a time, you will form lumps and spoil your sauce. If this happens, pass the sauce through a sieve.

4. Remove your pan from the stove for a few seconds and dribble in a little of the hot milk. Return the pan to the heat and stir briskly. Repeat this process, adding a little cream at the end if liked, until you have a smooth sauce similar in consistency to double cream.
5. Taste and adjust the seasoning if necessary.

CHEESE SAUCE (MORNAY)

I use freshly grated parmesan for cheese sauce. It is quite an expensive cheese but, having a strong taste, takes less to flavour the sauce and gives a lighter result. However, you may use cheddar or gruyere, but allow a little more. In this case, you will find that your sauce has a more elastic texture and care should be taken **not to add too much cheese** or it will become stringy.

PREPARATION AND METHOD

1. Make a béchamel sauce as on p.16, adding a little mustard powder at the same time as the flour (this is optional).
2. When the sauce is made, stir in 90gr/3oz of grated parmesan cheese (or 125gr /4oz of gruyere or cheddar) and cook gently until blended. Add a little cream.

—ooOoo—

MUSTARD SAUCE

Make a small quantity of béchamel sauce (see p.16) and stir in Dijon mustard to taste.

—ooOoo—

CAPER SAUCE

This simple sauce particularly complements the flavour of poached salmon and is an excellent alternative to Hollandaise Sauce.

TO SERVE 4 YOU WILL NEED

300ml /$^{1}/_{2}$pint Béchamel Sauce (p.16)
1 Tablespoon Capers
$^{1}/_{2}$ Teaspoon Caper Juice
$^{1}/_{2}$ Teaspoon Lemon Juice

PREPARATION AND METHOD

1. Make a béchamel sauce. If you have fish stock available, (see p,15) and you are serving the caper sauce with fish, use $^{1}/_{3}$ fish stock and $^{2}/_{3}$ milk to make the béchamel.
2. Put the béchamel in a bowl, add the caper juice and the lemon juice and stir in.
3. Finely chop the capers and add to the sauce **just before serving**.

—ooOoo—

WHITE SAUCE TO SERVE WITH VEGETABLES

This variation of béchamel sauce gives a very much lighter result than the more usual one made entirely from milk. Using vegetable water adds flavour and goodness. It is one of Auntie's secrets!

TO MAKE APPROX. 300ml/$^{1}/_{2}$pt YOU WILL NEED

30gr /1oz Unsalted Butter
30gr /1oz Plain Flour
300ml /$^{1}/_{2}$ pint Vegetable Cooking Water
A Little Milk
A Little Cream (optional)
Salt & Freshly Milled Black Pepper

METHOD
As for béchamel sauce p.16.

—ooOoo—

TOMATO SAUCE

(Sauce Provençale)

This sauce is very useful for dressing fish or vegetables, such as courgettes and marrow, and also for pasta dishes.

TOMATO SAUCE FREEZES WELL.

TO MAKE APPROX. 600ml /1 Pint YOU WILL NEED:

750gr /1¹/₂lb Ripe Tomatoes OR 800gr tin of Tomatoes
3 Medium Onions
1 Clove of Garlic
1 Teaspoon Herbes de Provence
1 Wine Glass /150ml White Wine
1 Wine Glass /150ml Water
1 Tablespoon Tomato Purée
2 Tablespoons Mild Olive Oil
1 Teaspoon Sugar
Salt & Freshly Milled Black Pepper

PREPARATION

❏ If you are using fresh tomatoes, make a small cross in the base of each tomato, place them in a bowl and cover with boiling water. Leave for 2 to 3 minutes, douse them with cold water and remove the skins, then chop into small chunks. (Or drain the tinned tomatoes, keeping the juice, and chop fairly small).

❏ Skin and chop the onions into small chunks.

❏ Skin, chop and crush the garlic.

METHOD

1. Heat the oil in a saucepan over a medium heat and cook the onion and garlic, without browning, until transparent.

2. Add the tomatoes, herbs, tomato juice and purée, wine and water. Bring to the boil and simmer for 20 minutes, stirring from time to time. Check the seasoning and add to taste.

3. Remove from the stove and liquidise or push through a sieve.

—ooOoo—

CHASSEUR SAUCE

Chasseur is a very useful sauce. It is very easy to make and stores well in the fridge for several days or CAN BE FROZEN. There is really no excuse for using a ready made product rather than making one with fresh ingredients!

Steak, turkey or chicken breasts sautéed and dressed with chasseur sauce make quick, tasty and easy meals. Real 'fast food'! There is a recipe for Pork Chasseur on p.141.

TO MAKE APPROX. 600ml /1 Pint YOU WILL NEED:

500gr /1lb White Mushrooms
500gr /1lb Tomatoes
2 Medium Onions
1 Clove of Garlic crushed
1 Tablespoon of Tomato Purée
1 Bay Leaf
Sprig of Parsley
1 Sprig of Thyme or ¹/₂tsp dried
300ml / ¹/₂pint White Wine

300ml /¹/₂ pint Chicken Stock*
45gr /1¹/₂ oz Unsalted Butter
Mild Olive Oil
Potato Flour

PREPARATION

❑ Cut a cross in the base of each tomato, put them in a bowl and pour boiling water over. Leave to soak for 2 to 3 minutes. Drain, plunge into cold water and remove the skins. Chop into small chunks.
❑ Wash and slice the mushrooms.
❑ Skin and cut the onions into small cubes.
   *If you have no fresh stock available, substitute ¹/₄ chicken cube dissolved in 300ml/¹/₂ pint boiling water.

METHOD

1. Melt the butter with a little oil in a saucepan on a medium heat. Add the onions and crushed garlic and cook gently until transparent, **not brown**.
2. Add the tomatoes, mushrooms, herbs, wine and stock. Simmer, stirring occasionally, for 20 minutes.
3. Mix a heaped teaspoon of potato flour with ¹/₃ cup of water. Add carefully to the sauce, **a little at a time**, stirring briskly, until the sauce has thickened. **Do not allow it to become too thick.**

When using chasseur sauce to dress meat dishes, **always add the meat juices from the sauté pan for added flavour.**

—ooOoo—

FRENCH DRESSING
(Vinaigrette)

There are various forms of French Dressing, many of which I find too strong or too sharp, tending to smother, rather than enhance, the flavours of a dish. This one, learned in Paris from "Auntie", is delicate and easy to make.

I prefer to use a French or Italian **cold pressed extra virgin olive oil**. Many olive oils tend to be very strong and pungent in flavour and, though a cold pressing is more expensive, I think it is well worth the extra. For those who do not like even this mild oil, groundnut oil can be used on its own.

FRENCH DRESSING WILL KEEP WELL IN A COOL PLACE FOR 2 TO 3 WEEKS.

TO MAKE APPROX. 300ml /¹/₂ Pint YOU WILL NEED:
75ml /2fl.oz Red Wine Vinegar
150ml /4fl. oz Olive Oil
225ml /6fl.oz Groundnut Oil
¹/₄ Teaspoon Dijon Mustard (optional)
¹/₂ Teaspoon Sugar
¹/₄ Teaspoon Salt
¹/₄ Teaspoon Freshly Milled Black Pepper

METHOD

1. Place all ingredients, except the oil, into a jug and mix thoroughly with a whisk.
2. Pour into a screw top bottle and shake vigorously.
3. Measure the oils into the jug and add to the

other ingredients in the bottle. Shake again to emulsify (mix thoroughly together).

USE with salads, asparagus, artichokes and hors d'oeuvre. **Always shake well before using.**
SECRET OF SUCCESS: the quality of your ingredients and correct seasoning.

—ooOoo—

MINT SAUCE

I find bottled mint sauce so sharp that it overpowers the flavour of lamb. As mint grows like a weed, to such an extent that it is best to plant it in a pot or bucket dug into the ground to prevent it taking over completely, it is easy and cheap to have a plentiful supply, even if you only have a small corner, pot or window box in which to plant it.

YOU CAN KEEP A SUPPLY OF CHOPPED MINT IN THE FREEZER for use when there is none in the garden.

YOU WILL NEED:
For every Tablespoon of Chopped Mint:
2 Tablespoons Boiling water
2 Tablespoons Malt or Red Wine Vinegar
Caster Sugar

PREPARATION & METHOD
1. Remove all the stalks from a bunch of fresh mint.
2. Place the leaves on a chopping board and liberally sprinkle with sugar. **This helps the chopping process and softens the sharp vinegar taste.** Take a large knife or cleaver and chop until fine.
3. Place the chopped mint in a bowl, add the boiling water and stir to dissolve the sugar. Add the vinegar and mix well.

—ooOoo—

MAYONNAISE

I was laboriously making mayonnaise in my hotel kitchen for forty-five guests when David, my chef, remarked that his daughter made mayonnaise with whole eggs in a food processor. It did not take me long to agree to an experiment and the result was so good that thereafter my whisking arm became redundant!

However, there will be times when you need only a little mayonnaise, or have no processor, so I will give both methods.

Do not attempt to make whole egg mayonnaise by hand, it won't work!

It is important when making mayonnaise that **all the ingredients are at a room temperature**, so take them out of the fridge in plenty of time.

TO MAKE APPROX. 300ml /¹/₂ Pint YOU WILL NEED:

2 Egg Yolks
1 Tablespoon White Wine Vinegar
OR half Vinegar, half Lemon Juice
250ml /9fl.oz Olive Oil OR Groundnut Oil OR a mixture of both
Pinch of Salt
Sprinkling of Ground Black Pepper

HAND METHOD

1. Separate the egg yolks. **Take care not to include any white**.
2. Place the yolks in a mixing bowl with a pinch of salt, a little sprinkling of pepper and the vinegar. Using a balloon whisk, mix together.

3. Place the bowl on a folded cloth to steady it, or wedge it in an open kitchen drawer (or ask some one to dribble in the oil for you). **Now comes the critical part!**
4. **Very slowly** dribble a little oil into the eggs, whisking briskly, **using a criss-cross action**. **Better be over cautious — just a drop or two at a time**. When the mixture starts to thicken, you can add the oil just a little faster, whisking all the time, so long as the oil is being absorbed into the mixture and not separating. Stop adding oil from time to time and give a little extra whisking.
    SHOULD YOUR MAYONNAISE SEPARATE, take another egg yolk in a separate bowl and whisk. Then, very slowly, add the separated mixture, whisking all the time, until it is absorbed. This should solve the problem!
    To test for consistency, dip your finger into the mixture and, if it forms an indentation, the mayonnaise is ready. You may like to add a little more vinegar or lemon at the end, depending on taste.

SECRET OF SUCCESS: don't be in a hurry. Add your oil very slowly. If you don't get this right, the mayonnaise will separate (see solution above).

—ooOoo—

FOOD PROCESSOR METHOD FOR MAKING MAYONNAISE

1. Separate the egg yolks as for the hand method, or use one whole egg. The result is lighter

and less dense than using yolks only. It is a matter of taste which recipe you prefer.

2. Place the egg yolks, or whole eggs, salt, pepper and vinegar into the food processor. Switch on and allow the ingredients to mix.

3. Through the funnel, **very slowly**, dribble in the oil.

   If you add the oil too fast, the mayonnaise may separate. In this case, remove the separated mixture from the food processor into a jug. Put another egg yolk into the machine and give it a short spin. With the machine switched on, **very slowly** pour in the separated mixture, until it has been absorbed. This should solve the problem!

4. When the mayonnaise has reached a nice thick, creamy consistency, switch the machine off and test with your finger. If it leaves an indentation the mayonnaise is ready.

   Should you wish, you may whisk in a little more vinegar or lemon at the end.

—ooOoo—

SACHET OF SPICES OR CLOVES

Use a square of muslin and string or, better still, I have devised a quicker and very simple method by using tubular finger bandage!

Stretch a length of bandage over the applicator and fill with the required quantity of spice, pull the bandage up and tie a knot, turn upside down and tie a knot at the other end, sealing the spice in a sachet.

—ooOoo—

TARTARE SAUCE

This sauce uses mayonnaise (preferably fresh home-made) as its base and is served with fried or grilled fish and fish cakes.

I use sweet gherkins. Those without sugar make a very sharp sauce. **Look on the label for the inclusion of sugar in the ingredients.**

TO MAKE APPROX. 150ml /$^1/_4$ Pint YOU WILL NEED:
150ml /$^1/_4$ pint of Mayonnaise
1 Heaped Tablespoon Finely Chopped Onion or Shallot
1 Heaped Tablespoon Finely Chopped Gherkin
1 Heaped Tablespoon Finely Chopped Capers
$^1/_2$ Tablespoon Finely Chopped Fresh Parsley
Juice of $^1/_4$ Lemon

METHOD
Place all the ingredients in a bowl and stir to mix.

—ooOoo—

SEAFOOD DRESSING

This sauce should be pink and not red! How often a prawn cocktail is spoilt by a strong, sharp sauce, seemingly designed to kill any delicate seafood flavour!

This is a simple and quick way to make a delicate sauce, using home-made mayonnaise (see p. 22)

TO MAKE APPROX. 300ml /¹/₂ Pint YOU WILL NEED:

300ml /¹/₂ pint Home-made Mayonnaise
¹/₂ Tablespoon Tomato Ketchup
1 Teaspoon Lemon Juice
1 Tablespoon Brandy
A Pinch of Cayenne Pepper

METHOD

Take all the ingredients and gently mix them well together.

Use for dressing prawns in hors d'oeuvres and for prawn cocktail.

—ooOoo—

BÉARNAISE SAUCE

This sauce is better made with fresh herbs, but a good result can be achieved with dried, if care is taken not to use too much.

If you use a shallow mixing bowl set over a large saucepan of water, this will give you plenty of room to whisk, making the process easier.

Béarnaise sauce can be served with steaks, chateaubriand and roast beef.

TO MAKE APPROX. 300ml /¹/₂ Pint YOU WILL NEED:

3 Egg Yolks
185gr /6oz Unsalted Butter
75ml /2¹/₂ fl.oz Dry White Wine
2 Tablespoons White Wine Vinegar
1 Tablespoon Water
1 Tablespoon Fresh Chopped Tarragon or 1 tsp dried
1 Tablespoon Fresh Chopped Chervil or ¹/₂ tsp dried
¹/₂ Fresh Bay Leaf or Fragment of Dried
6 Peppercorns
¹/₂ Teaspoon of Salt

METHOD

1. Melt the butter in a saucepan and set aside until lukewarm.
2. In another saucepan, boil together the chervil and bay leaf, peppercorns, wine, vinegar, salt and **half** the tarragon, until reduced to about one third (about 2 tablespoons).
3. Strain this liquid through a sieve into a mixing bowl.

4. In another bowl, separate the egg yolks, discarding the whites, add the water and whisk together.
5. Combine the strained liquid and the egg yolks and place the bowl over a saucepan of simmering water. Whisk continuously until it begins to thicken.
    Do not allow your sauce to get too hot. If in danger of becoming so, remove the saucepan from the heat.
6. **Very slowly** dribble in the melted butter, whisking continuously, until the sauce is a thick, creamy consistency.
7. To finish, add the rest of the chopped tarragon. The sauce can be covered and kept hot, in the basin over warm water, until you are ready to use it.

SECRET OF SUCCESS: don't let your sauce get too hot during making. Start adding the butter **before** the egg mix gets too thick, or it will not mix in.

—ooOoo—

HOLLANDAISE SAUCE

This delicate sauce is perfect with poached fish, particularly salmon. It also goes well with eggs and vegetables, especially asparagus.

Hollandaise is not an easy sauce to make, but practice will make perfect! **It is very important not to get the sauce too hot whilst making,** or it will separate.

Use a shallow mixing bowl over a large saucepan. This will give you plenty of room to whisk and make your task easier.

TO MAKE APPROX. 300ml /$^{1}/_{2}$ Pint YOU WILL NEED:

3 Egg Yolks
1 Tablespoon White Wine Vinegar
Water
8 Black Peppercorns
185gr /6oz Unsalted Butter
Pinch of Salt

METHOD
1. Melt the butter in a saucepan and put on one side until lukewarm.
2. Put the peppercorns in a small saucepan with the vinegar, 3 tablespoons of water and a pinch of salt. Boil until the liquid has reduced to 1 tablespoon. **Be careful that it does not boil dry.** Don't turn your back on it!
3. Strain the liquid through a sieve into a mixing bowl set over a pan of simmering water.
4. In another bowl, separate the egg yolks,

discarding the whites, add 1 tablespoon of water and whisk together.

5. Combine the strained liquid and the egg yolks and place the bowl over a saucepan of simmering water. Whisk continuously until it begins to thicken.

    Do not allow your sauce to become too hot. If there is a danger of this, remove the pan from the heat.

6. **Very slowly** dribble the melted butter into the egg mixture, whisking all the time, until your sauce is a nice thick, creamy consistency.

    You can keep hollandaise hot in the bowl over warm water, covered, until you are ready to use it.

SECRET OF SUCCESS: start dribbling the melted butter into the sauce **as soon as it starts to thicken**. To delay at this stage will cause the eggs to become too solid for the butter to blend in. Better too soon than too late!

—ooOoo—

CLARIFIED BUTTER

This is not a sauce, but a very useful item to keep in your fridge. 'Clarifying' butter separates the milky content from the fat. It is the milky content that causes butter to burn when you are frying, so clarified butter, when used for frying, **will not burn**. When using clarified butter for frying you need not add oil.

You can clarify the butter either in a saucepan or the microwave.

YOU WILL NEED:
250gr /8oz Unsalted Butter
600ml/1 pint Water

SAUCEPAN METHOD

1. Cut a packet of unsalted butter into 6 or 8 pieces and place in a saucepan with the water. Slowly heat until the butter is thoroughly melted.
2. Pour the mixture into a bowl and chill in the fridge until the fat solidifies.
3. Remove the piece of solid fat and scrape the milk off the underside.
4. Wrap in foil and keep until required in the fridge.

MICROWAVE METHOD

1. Put the unsalted butter and the water in a bowl. Microwave until the butter is thoroughly melted.
2. Pour the mixture into a bowl and chill in the fridge until the fat solidifies.

    Then as 3 and 4 above.

—ooOoo—

SOUPS & BROTH

introduction to methods and recipes

SOUPS & BROTHS

Soup making is probably the easiest form of cooking to master. The preparation time is minimal and they are economical to produce, tasty and nourishing to eat. In fact, soups are so easy, cheap and quick to make I wonder why so many tins and packets are sold!

Trimmings from vegetables and bones from meat and poultry can be used to make soup stock. Keep the outside leaves of leeks and the trimmings of celery. Do not discard the bones and trimmings from a joint or chicken — just boil them with a little chicken cube to form the basis of a soup, which can be kept in the freezer until required (see Section 3 for making quick stocks).

When making soups, I suggest making more than actually required, allowing for a useful reserve in the freezer for occasions when time is at a premium.

For many vegetable soups I do not use stock or herbs because, though tasty, they tend to have a sameness about them which detracts from the freshness of the more subtle vegetable flavour. This also pleases vegetarians!

Under the heading of broth, you can make a variety of 'potages', each with a distinctive flavour derived from the stock used.

All broths are made with similar vegetable ingredients and the same method. The exact quantities of vegetables are not crucial and very successful results will be obtained with slight variations dictated by availability.

Any pan of suitable size will do a good job for making broth, but for thick or cream soups you will find a cast iron casserole, because of its superior heat distribution, less likely to catch or burn, so requiring less attention. It can also be taken to the table and double as a tureen.

—ooOoo—

CREAM OF MUSHROOM SOUP

For this soup I recommend using white or button mushrooms, as the flat field variety produce a grey and rather unattractive colour.

TO SERVE 4 YOU WILL NEED:

1 Medium Onion
375gr /12oz White Mushrooms
60gr /2oz Unsalted Butter
60gr /2oz Plain Flour
150ml /¹/₄ pint Double Cream
Approx. 900ml /1¹/₂ pints Boiling Water
Salt & freshly Milled Black Pepper

PREPARATION

❑ Have a kettle of boiling water handy.
❑ Wash and slice the mushrooms.
❑ Halve the onion, remove the skin and cut into small chunks.

METHOD

1. Melt the butter in a saucepan over a low heat.

2. Add the onion and mushrooms and cook gently for 2 to 3 minutes. **Do not brown**.

3. Removing the pan from the heat, add the flour and stir vigorously to form a roux or paste.

4. Gradually add the boiling water, a little at a time, stirring continuously to avoid lumps, until you have the consistency of thin cream. Return the pan to the heat.

5. Add a little salt, **not too much** or, after cooking, you may get too salty a result. Allow to simmer for 30 minutes, stirring from time to time.

6. Pass though a food processor or liquidiser, but take care not to over-process, as you do not want a completely smooth result. **The texture of the soup is improved if particles of mushroom remain**.

7. When ready to serve, check the seasoning and stir in the cream.

SECRET OF SUCCESS: is to get the texture and seasoning right.

—ooOoo—

CREAM OF TOMATO SOUP

I suppose cream of tomato is the most popular of all soups, hence its widespread production in tinned or packet form. Freshly made soup, however, always has the edge over the manufactured variety, besides being full of nourishment and containing no preservatives or colour.

Tomato soup is easy to make and STORES WELL IN THE FREEZER.

TO SERVE 6 TO 8 YOU WILL NEED:

750gr /1¹/₂lb Ripe Tomatoes*
      OR 800gr tin of Italian Tomatoes
2 Medium Onions
3 Carrots
2 Sticks of Celery
1 Large or 2 Small Garlic Cloves (crushed)
2 Small Bay Leaves
90gr /3oz Unsalted Butter
90gr /3oz Plain Flour
2 Tablespoons Tomato Purée
Water
75ml /2¹/₂ fl.oz Cream
Salt & Freshly Milled Black Pepper
* (If using fresh tomatoes) Sugar

PREPARATION
- Put a kettle on to boil and keep it handy.
- Halve the onions then skin and cut into small chunks.
- Peel and slice the carrots.
- Wash and chop the celery.
- Chop the tomatoes finely. **No need to skin them.** If using tinned tomatoes, strain off the liquid and set it aside.

METHOD
1. Melt the butter in a saucepan and add the onion, carrot, celery and garlic. Cook slowly over a low to medium heat for 2 to 3 minutes, stirring to keep from browning.
2. Remove the pan from the heat while you stir in the flour. Then cook for 2 to 3 minutes, **stirring vigorously.**
3. Chop the tomatoes and add to the saucepan. **If you are using fresh tomatoes, add 1 tablespoon of sugar.**
4. Add the bay leaves and stir in the tomato puree.
5. Gradually add boiling water (and the liquid from the tinned tomatoes if used), **stirring briskly** to avoid lumps forming (if lumps threaten, remove the pan from the heat and return it when the liquid has blended smoothly in). Continue to achieve a good consistency, neither too thick nor too thin.
6. Simmer for ¹/₂ hour **without a lid**, stirring from time to time to prevent sticking or burning.
7. Liquidise or pass through a food processor and then strain through a sieve, using a pastry brush. Season to taste and stir in the cream **just before serving.**

CREAM OF CHICKEN SOUP

Ask your butcher for chicken carcasses to make the stock. Or buy a whole chicken and slice off the two breasts to use in another dish, i.e. Chicken Breasts in Cream and Sherry Sauce p.139, or Chicken Breasts with Garlic, Mushrooms and Red Wine Sauce p.138.

ALLOW ONE HOUR TO MAKE YOUR STOCK IN ADVANCE.

TO SERVE 6 TO 8 YOU WILL NEED:
INGREDIENTS
3 Chicken Carcasses
OR 1 Chicken without the breasts
2 Medium Onions
60gr /2oz Unsalted Butter
60gr /2oz Plain Flour
150ml /¹/₄ pint Cream
Salt & Freshly Milled Black Pepper

TO MAKE THE STOCK
Boil the chicken or carcasses in 3 pints of water. Do not boil fast, just simmer, **without a lid**, for one hour.

PREPARATION FOR THE SOUP
❏ Strain off the stock and allow the carcasses to cool.
❏ Pick off the lean meat, chop finely and set aside.
❏ Halve, skin and finely chop the onion.

METHOD
1. Melt the butter in a saucepan and sweat over a medium heat, stirring to prevent browning, for 3 to 5 minutes.
2. Add the flour, **stirring vigorously** with a wooden spoon, to form a roux. Cook for 2 to 3 minutes.
3. Add the **hot** chicken stock, starting with just a dribble, and stirring vigorously, until you have the consistency of single cream. (If necessary, remove the pan from the heat while stirring in the liquid, to prevent lumps forming).
4. Simmer for 30 minutes, **without a lid**, stirring from time to time to prevent burning. If you need more liquid to thin the soup, use milk.
5. Add the chopped chicken and pass through a liquidiser or food processor, taking care not to over-process and **leaving some particles of chicken**.
6. Season with salt and freshly milled black pepper to taste..

TO SERVE: Reheat and stir in the cream.

—ooOoo—

POTATO SOUP
with Croutons

This soup needs chicken stock, fresh or cube. It is very quick and easy to make.

If you are using fresh chicken stock, either **allow 1 hour to make it** (see p.15), or take some from the freezer **in time to thaw**.

TO SERVE 6 TO 8 YOU WILL NEED:

1k /2lb Old Potatoes
2 Medium Onions
1500ml /2¹/₂ pints Chicken Stock
60gr /2oz Unsalted Butter
150ml /¹/₄ pint Cream
300ml /¹/₂ pint Milk
Freshly Ground Nutmeg
Salt & Freshly Milled Black Pepper
Bread and Clarified Butter *(p.26) or
Mild Olive Oil to make croutons for garnish
Freshly Chopped Parsley Garnish

PREPARATION

❏ Prepare your chicken stock as on page 15. Or make a stock with 1 cube and 1500ml /2¹/₂ pints of boiling water.
❏ Halve, skin and cut the onions into small chunks.
❏ Peel and slice the potatoes.

METHOD

1. Melt the butter in a cast iron casserole or saucepan. Add the potato and onion and sweat over a medium heat, stirring to prevent browning, for 3 to 5 minutes.
2. Add the stock and simmer, without a lid, for 30 minutes.

MEANWHILE MAKE THE CROUTONS

Cut one or two slices of bread, remove the crusts and cut into small cubes. Heat a knob of butter (preferably clarified) or oil in a frying pan on medium heat. ***Clarified butter does not burn so achieves a better result**. Fry the croutons until golden brown.

TO FINISH THE SOUP

3. Check for seasoning and sprinkle with freshly ground nutmeg.
4. Liquidise until fine and creamy in texture, or sieve.
5. Return to the pan and bring back to heat, add the milk and, if necessary, a little extra water. **The texture should not be too thick and stodgy.**
6. Add the cream and check the seasoning.

SERVE with a sprinkle of fresh chopped parsley and croutons.

SECRET OF SUCCESS: the nutmeg gives this soup its distinctive flavour, but be careful not to use too much for it can be overpowering. The effect desired is so delicate that you hardly know it's there!

LEEK & POTATO SOUP

(Vichyssoise)

Vichyssoise is a very popular chilled summer soup, but it is equally delicious served hot. Aunt Louise, in Paris, used to serve it as a simple leek and potato soup, finished with a generous knob of butter - no milk or cream!

Be careful not to overcook this soup and lose the pretty pale green colour.

TO SERVE 6 TO 8 YOU WILL NEED:

500gr /1lb Old Potatoes
750gr /1¹/₂ lb Leeks
1 Medium Onion
60gr /2oz Unsalted Butter
1500ml /2¹/₂ pints Water
300ml /¹/₂ pint Milk
150ml /¹/₄ pint Cream
Salt & Freshly Milled Black Pepper

PREPARATION

❏ Put a kettle on to boil.
❏ Peel and thinly slice the potatoes.
❏ Halve, skin and finely chop the onion.
❏ Remove any very tough or discoloured outside leaves from the leeks, but **use all the fresh green as this adds colour to the soup**, then thoroughly wash them, **upside down** under running cold water and cut into small chunks.

METHOD

1. Melt the butter in a saucepan and sweat the vegetables (slowly cook) on a low heat for 3 to 5 minutes, stirring to prevent browning.
2. Add the boiling water and a little salt. Leave to simmer for 25 minutes, **without a lid**.
3. Add the milk and liquidise — **not too smooth**.
4. Return to the pan, check the seasoning and, when ready to serve, reheat and stir in the cream.

SECRET OF SUCCESS: do not overblend the soup, or you will spoil the texture.

—ooOoo—

CARROT SOUP

(Potage Crecy)

This recipe is a variation of Potage Crecy. Made without stock, it is a very delicate, vegetarian soup. See illustration p.37.

TO SERVE 6 TO 8 YOU WILL NEED:

750gr /1¹/₂ lb Carrots
500gr /1lb Potatoes
2 Medium Onions
1500ml /2¹/₂ pints Water
90gr /3oz Unsalted Butter
1 Tablespoon Sugar
Salt & Freshly Milled Black Pepper
Freshly Chopped Parsley to Garnish

PREPARATION

❏ Wash, peel and cut the potatoes and carrots into small chunks.
❏ Halve, skin and cut the onions into small chunks.

METHOD

1. Melt half the butter in the saucepan and sweat the vegetables over a medium heat, stirring to prevent browning.
2. Add the water, season with salt and black pepper and add the sugar. Simmer for 25 minutes **with out a lid**.
3. Carefully pass through a liquidiser or food processor to achieve a texture in which **some particles of carrot remain**, adding a little extra water if necessary.
4. To finish the soup, reheat it, stirring in the rest of the butter. Check the seasoning and sprinkle with parsley to serve.
   Carrot soup is inclined to settle, so **stir it as you ladle it out**.

—ooOoo—

WATERCRESS SOUP

Watercress soup has a lovely 'bite' to it and is a pretty colour, but it **will not keep its colour or country freshness for more than a few hours**. It is not a soup for the deepfreeze.

It is one of the vegetable soups which is an exception to the 'no stock' rule. It uses chicken stock, so either have this made in advance (see p.15), or ALLOW AN HOUR TO MAKE IT. If no fresh stock is available, use one chicken stock cube to 1500 ml/2 $^{1}/_{2}$ pints of water.

TO SERVE 6 TO 8 YOU WILL NEED:
1k /2lb Old Potatoes
2 Medium Onions
2 Bunches of Fresh Watercress
1500ml /2$^{1}/_{2}$ pints Chicken Stock
30gr /2oz Unsalted Butter
300ml /$^{1}/_{2}$ pint Milk
150ml /$^{1}/_{4}$ pint Cream
Cayenne Pepper
Salt & Freshly Milled Black Pepper

PREPARATION
❑ Peel and slice the potatoes.
❑ Halve, skin and cut the onions into small chunks.
❑ Trim any roots from the watercress, wash it very thoroughly and chop up roughly.

METHOD

1. Melt the butter in the saucepan, add the potato and onion and sweat over a medium heat, stirring to prevent browning, for 2 to 3 minutes.
2. Add the stock, bring to the boil and simmer, **with out a lid**, for 25 minutes.
3. Add the watercress to the boiling soup and cook for 3 minutes, **without a lid**.
4. Add the milk and a sprinkle of cayenne pepper.
5. Liquidise carefully, **leaving small particles of watercress**.

TO SERVE : reheat the soup, check the seasoning and stir in the cream.
SECRET OF SUCCESS: is not to overcook, or you will lose the delicate green colour.

FRENCH ONION SOUP

French onion soup is the essence of France and always beckons me to return! It is wonderfully warming and, with hot cheesy croutons of French bread floating on top, is a meal in itself!

Its basis is a really good stock, preferably made from veal bones but, as these are not readily available, you can use beef marrow bones (see p.15).

Make your stock in advance, have it ready in the freezer and take it out in time to thaw, or allow 3 hours to make it.

TO SERVE 6 TO 8 YOU WILL NEED:

1k /2lb Onions
2 Cloves of Garlic
1 Bay Leaf
1500ml /2¹/₂pints Beef Stock
300ml /¹/₂ pint Red Wine
Unsalted Butter
Mild Olive Oil
Sugar
French Bread for Croutons
Gruyere for Garnish
Salt & Freshly Milled Black Pepper

METHOD AND PREPARATION

1. Halve the onion, remove the skin and slice thinly.
2. Crush the garlic.
3. Heat a couple of knobs of butter with a little oil in a large frying pan and fry the onions in batches. **Do not overload the pan** or the onions will not brown easily. Fry until brown but not burnt!

4. Transfer the browned onions and garlic to a large saucepan and add the stock, bay leaves and wine. Rinse the frying pan and add the juices so as not to waste them.
5. Simmer **without a lid** for 3 hours. Add water from time to time to maintain the original quantity. Season to taste.
Onion soup improves with long cooking.

MEANWHILE PREPARE THE CROUTONS :
Cut a French stick into slices about the thickness of your finger, or pieces of bread of equivalent size, allowing one per person. Dry them under a slow grill or in a hot oven.

TO SERVE :
divide the soup into deep heatproof bowls, put a crouton in each and sprinkle with grated gruyere. Place under a hot grill until the cheese is bubbling.

YELLOW PEA SOUP

(Crème Egyptienne)

I can only imagine that this soup got its French name from its sand colour!

A wonderful soup for a winter's day, it is for me a wonderful soup for any day! A real favourite and **so** easy to make!

The essential ingredient is ham stock so, whenever you cook a ham or bacon joint, make it an opportunity to have yellow pea soup, or keep the stock and save it in the freezer. If the stock is very salty, use part stock and part water.

TO SERVE 6 TO 8 YOU WILL NEED:

1500ml /2¹/₂ pints Ham Stock
250gr /8oz Yellow Split Peas
1 Medium Onion
2 Carrots
2 Sticks of Celery
Freshly Milled Black Pepper
Cream (optional)
Croutons (see p.32 Potato Soup) to Garnish

PREPARATION AND METHOD

1. Peel and chop the vegetables.
2. Put all the vegetables in a saucepan, add the stock and the peas, bring the boil and simmer for 2 hours, **without a lid**, stirring occasionally to prevent sticking and burning.
3. Allow to cool a little and then liquidise until smooth. The texture should be about that of single cream.

TO SERVE : reheat, check the seasoning, adding freshly milled black pepper if necessary and a little cream if liked. Sprinkle each serving with a tablespoon of croutons.

—ooOoo—
SCOTCH BROTH

This is my favourite broth, which I often make from the leftovers of a roast leg or shoulder of lamb, with the addition of a little chicken cube. But the fresh meat recipe which follows gives the best flavour.

Ask your butcher for a jointed neck of lamb.

TO SERVE 6 TO 8 YOU WILL NEED:

500gr /1lb Neck of Lamb
1500ml /2¹/₂ pints Water
1 Large Onion
1 Leek
3 Medium Carrots
2 Sticks of Celery
2 Medium Potatoes
60gr /2oz Pearl Barley
1 Bay Leaf
Salt & Freshly Milled Black Pepper

PREPARATION AND METHOD

1. Trim all surplus skin and fat from the pieces of lamb.
2. Place the lamb in a large saucepan with the water and a bay leaf. Bring to the boil.
3. Skim off the scum with a spoon. Add the barley and leave to simmer.
4. Wash, peel and chop the vegetables into small dice and add to the pot with about ¹/₂ teaspoon of salt. Simmer for 2 hours.
5. Remove the lamb with a slotted spoon and strip the meat from the bones, discarding any fat, gristle or bones. Finely chop the lean meat and return this to the pot.

TO SERVE : check the seasoning and reheat the broth. Decorate with freshly chopped parsley.

—ooOoo—

Carrot Soup
Recipe p.33

VEGETABLES & SALADS

General principles of preparation
and cooking with recipes

GENERAL PRINCIPLES FOR COOKING VEGETABLES

Happily, overcooked vegetables are mostly a thing of the past, although sometimes the pendulum has swung to the other extreme and they are served half raw. I like my vegetables cooked but firm.

I learnt a great many wonderful tips from my late wife's French aunt in Paris, who was probably the best cook I have ever known. Her easy-to-remember golden rule for boiling vegetables was :

1. **"Everything that grows above the ground — lid off!"** (which preserves the colour)
2. **"Everything that grows below the ground — lid on!"** (this speeds the cooking and there is no problem with the colour.)

Wash green vegetables in plenty of fresh water.

There is a school of thought that green vegetables should be cooked in the minimum of water to preserve the goodness. I disagree because, placed in only a little water, vegetables go off the boil and take longer to return to temperature. Plunging into plenty of fast boiling water 'seals' the vegetables and cooking is speeded up, thus producing better colour and flavour and retaining more of the essential vitamins and minerals. You will find a cast iron saucepan, due to its superior heat retention, will aid the speed at which the water returns to boiling.

To see when vegetables are ready, test with a small pointed knife.

When possible, **avoid preparing vegetables too long in advance and cut them as little as possible**. Once cut, they 'bleed' and start to loose their flavour. If it is necessary to prepare and cook in advance, reheating in the microwave gives a better result than keeping hot. Kept hot, vegetables lose their colour and become over-strong in flavour. (N.B. Take care, however, not to over microwave).

I have a useful tip for crisping up green vegetables or salad. In hot weather cabbage, spinach, greens and lettuce look sad and limp. To bring them back to life, wash and prepare them, shake off excess water and put them in a saucepan or basin. Cover and leave for 2 to 3 hours, or overnight and they will come up fresh and smiling again.

Seasoning is one of the most important aspects in cooking vegetables and getting it right needs practice. When adding salt to your pot **always measure by eye**, pouring the salt into the palm of your hand or using a spoon. **Green vegetables require more salt than root vegetables** because they are cooked very quickly and so do not absorb so much salt. As a starting guide, use about 2 teaspoons to approximately $2\frac{1}{2}$ litres /4 pints of water and adjust to suit you own taste.

The basic preparation of all root vegetables is the same – wash, peel and cut up, except for potatoes, which are sometimes cooked in their skins.

French Salads
Recipe p.57

Preparing Leeks
Recipe p.46

If you have stainless steel saucepans, **wait until the water is boiling before adding salt.** When put into cold water, salt will leave white spots, which in time can eat into the surface of the pan.

When draining green vegetables, except peas and beans, **lift them from the water with a perforated spoon into a colander to drain,** rather than tipping them from the pan. This will ensure that any grit overlooked in the washing will be left behind in the water.

Most vegetables can be served plain or with a little added butter. I use a pastry brush to paint them with melted butter, which gives them a nice sheen, without too much butter to mask the flavour. I use fresh chopped parsley to garnish many vegetables, so I always keep some handy.

One more word of advice. **Keep it simple!** Many people, especially when entertaining, feel it necessary to serve a large number of vegetables. One, or at most two, perfectly cooked, better complements the main dish and has more eye appeal when served. The most memorable meals are usually the least pretentious.

—ooOoo—

GREEN VEGETABLES

Remember — lid off to retain the colour.

—ooOoo—

CABBAGE

❑ Remove the outer coarse leaves.
❑ Slice the cabbage in two and then into two or three, depending on size.
❑ Remove any thick stem.
❑ Boil for 5 to 6 minutes, turning it over and pushing down into the water to ensure even cooking, and **lift out with perforated spoon** into a colander. Chop with a cabbage cutter or sharp knife.

Serve as soon as possible, since **cabbage soon loses its fresh-cooked flavour.** It is delicious served plain, or it can be returned to the pan, tossed in a little unsalted butter and seasoned with freshly milled black pepper.

The reason for cooking cabbage in large pieces and cutting afterwards is that, with this method, it will 'bleed' less and retain a better colour, texture and flavour.

BRUSSELS SPROUTS

❑ Choose small, bright green sprouts of fairly uniform size, and trim each sprout by removing the stem and outside leaves, then cut a cross in the base of each to assist cooking.
❑ Boil for 6-8 minutes.

NOTE : if you are reheating sprouts in a microwave, **take care to use a low heat,** for they are inclined to burst and make an awful mess!

CAULIFLOWER

A fresh cauliflower is firm and tight looking and should be a creamy white.

- ❑ Halve or quarter, removing the large parts of stem, then **soak for 5 to 10 minutes in lightly salted water** to bring out any small bugs that might be lurking in the flowers and rinse thoroughly.
- ❑ Cook for 6 to 8 minutes.

Serve either plain or with a white sauce **using the vegetable water** (see p.18).

BROCCOLI/CALABRESE

Choose tight, dark green heads.

- ❑ Remove the base of the thick stalk and divide the head into 4 or 6, then make a cut into the stalk of each piece, to ensure that it cooks as quickly as the flower and boil for 3 or 4 minutes.

Be careful not to overcook.
Serve plain or dressed with a white sauce, **using the vegetable water**, as for cauliflower, (see p.18).

—ooOoo—

SPINACH

Baby leaf spinach is fine for salads, but for cooking I much prefer large leaf spinach — it has more body and flavour. It also has quite a lot of grit and mud on its leaves, so requires careful washing! Spinach boils down a lot in cooking, so make sure you have enough, allow about 250gr/8oz of unprepared spinach per person.

- ❑ Fold the leaf and tear away the stalk.
- ❑ Wash thoroughly in a sink full of cold water, lifting the spinach out, to leave any grit and earth behind. Repeat three or four times, until clean.
- ❑ Shake off the surplus water and drop into a large pan of fast boiling **well salted** water. To cook, just bring back to the boil, turning with a perforated spoon.

It is particularly important with spinach to **lift out into a colander with a perforated spoon**, so any grit missed in washing will remain in the cooking water. Press the excess water out with the perforated spoon and cut up with a cabbage cutter or sharp knife.

To serve, return the spinach to the (rinsed) saucepan with a little melted butter and season with freshly milled black pepper. Spinach is particularly good with fish.

NOTE : I always cook more than I need and then wrap individual portions in cling film and put them into the freezer for 'Florentine' dishes — very useful when time is short.

*Fresh Vegetables
for Ratatouille*
Recipe p.54

Brandade Parisienne
Recipe p.75

LEEKS

I am pleased when I see leeks sold, as in France, with plenty of green top, for this is just as delicious as the white! Choose young leeks, about 2.5cm (1") thick.

❑ Strip off any coarse outside leaves and cut off any brown root leaving enough green to form about one third of the length.

❑ Lay the leeks on your chopping board and slit each lengthways from halfway down the white to the end of the green, then wash thoroughly under cold running water **holding the leek upside down** to ensure that all the grit is washed out and not further into the base of the leek!

❑ Tie three or four leeks together into bundles with string at the top and bottom and then cut each bundle into two. See illustration p.41. This may seem a fiddle, but it makes for easier handling and neater serving. They can also, when required, be easily cut again into shorter lengths.

❑ Cook for 4 to 5 minutes, then remove from the pan with a perforated spoon or tongs and drain in a colander. Remove the string.

Leeks are best served plain with sauce dishes and casseroles. With roasts and grills they are delicious in a white sauce **made with the cooking water** (see p.18).

FRENCH OR KENYA BEANS

These are now imported and obtainable for most of the year.

❑ The quickest way of 'topping and tailing' these beans is to do a small bunch at a time, with a sharp cook's knife, cutting downwards onto a chopping board. They can then be left whole or cut in half, as preferred.

❑ Cooking time will vary according to the thickness of the beans, so after 4 minutes remove and test one.

NOTE: if you are cooking beans in advance, strain into a colander and then douse with cold water (known as 'refreshing') to retain their colour and flavour. Reheat when required in a microwave or in a saucepan with butter.

RUNNER BEANS

These beans have a really distinctive flavour and are a favourite with everyone.

❑ Choose nice bright, firm beans. Spanish flat beans are lighter in colour, but very good and are prepared and cooked in the same way.

❑ Cut off the tops and tails and the strings down the sides. If you find a bean with a tough interior skin, discard it, as one stringy bean can spoil the whole pot!

❑ You can either coarse-cut the beans diagonally or shred them. I think they retain more flavour when coarse-cut.

❑ Cook for 5 minutes.
Serve plain or brushed with melted butter.

BROAD BEANS

What a pity broad beans have such a very short season! They are a most wonderful treat when eaten young, but unfortunately go tough with age. It is a little tedious removing the beans from the pod, but well worth the effort!

❑ Cook for 3 to 5 minutes.

Serve plain or lightly brushed with melted butter.

PEAS

Choose bright green, smooth pods which are **not too full**. Like all vegetables, they are very much better when young.

❑ Cook for 4 to 5 minutes. A sprig of fresh mint added to the water gives a lovely fresh taste.

Serve plain or brushed with a little melted butter.

CELERY

Celery is very versatile, it can be used chopped raw in salads, served in small sticks with cheese or as part of "crudités" with a dip, added to many casseroles and soups or cooked as a vegetable.

I prefer to boil, rather than braise, celery when using it as a vegetable. This way it retains its delicate flavour and is also much quicker and easier!

It is important to prepare celery carefully.

❑ Break off the outside sticks and save these for soup or casseroles, then slice off any brown on the root end, retaining as much of the root as possible, as **this is particularly sweet**.

❑ Cut into three, discarding the top section and cut the base or heart end lengthways into four or six.

❑ With small sharp knife or peeler, remove the stringy outer parts of the stems.

❑ Wash thoroughly and tie into bundles.

❑ Cook for 6 to 7 minutes, **with a lid on! (This is the exception to prove the rule!)**

Serve brushed with melted butter and freshly milled black pepper.

COURGETTES

Courgettes are available all the year round. Choose those that are crisp and shiny. They are easy and quick to prepare. They are also **very easy to overcook!** So beware! **Courgettes spoil if kept hot, so cook them at the last minute**.

❑ With small courgettes, slice off the tip and cut into thick disks. Discard the stalk end, as this is bitter. For larger courgettes, cut off each end, cut in half and then slice each half lengthways into four or six pieces.

❑ Cook for 2 to 3 minutes.

❑ Return the courgettes to the saucepan and coat with a little melted butter to serve.

47

French Country Paté
Recipe p.68

ASPARAGUS

There are two varieties of asparagus, white and green which are both delicious. Always a treat as a vegetable or, eaten on its own, as a starter or light meal.

❏ Choose medium thick, fresh looking stems with tight heads. Cut off the ends and give them a drink by standing in a jug of cold water for an hour or so before cooking.

❏ Scrape or peel the lower part of the stems and, using thin string, tie into bundles of 6 or 8 stems.

❏ If you have an asparagus kettle it is excellent for cooking white asparagus, which requires more cooking time than the green variety. The design allows the stems to cook in boiling water and the tips to cook in the steam, with the lid on. But for green asparagus I recommend you use sufficient boiling water to cover the tips of the asparagus **and leave the lid off.** Alternatively use a large saucepan without a lid.

❏ Cook the asparagus for 6 to 8 minutes.

Eaten on its own asparagus can be served hot with melted butter or cold (better still, just tepid) with French dressing (see p.20).

GLOBE ARTICHOKES

Artichokes, for me, are the caviar of vegetables! When faced with one to eat for the first time they can present quite a puzzle! However, armed with a finger bowl of warm water to rinse messy fingers, large table napkin and a spare dish for the pieces, they really pose no problem.

Picking off each petal, dunking it in the sauce and scraping off the flesh with your teeth may not sound very elegant, but artichokes are a wonderfully informal starter and icebreaker, or complete light meal. When you reach the very small petals at the centre, discard these, together with the hairy mound in the middle, which is inedible. Underneath you will find the heart, the pearl in the oyster, which you can eat with a knife and fork.

❏ **Do not remove the stem until you are ready to use the artichokes**, or the heart will turn brown.

❏ Place the chokes in a bowl of cold salted water for a few minutes, to flush out any foreign bodies!

❏ Fast boil for 35 to 40 minutes, **without a lid** and not too much salt, as with a long cooking time they will absorb plenty.

❏ To test, lift out one artichoke and pull off a petal.Drain **UPSIDE DOWN** in a colander.

Serve hot with melted butter or cold (**for perfection just tepid!**) with French dressing (see p.20).

ROOT VEGETABLES

The basic preparation of all root vegetables is the same — wash, peel and cut up — except for potatoes, which are sometimes cooked in their skins. All root vegetables should be cooked with the lid on.

ONIONS

When a young commis chef applies to join a commercial kitchen 'Brigade', he is often set a test by the chef to assess his ability. This invariably consists of making a béchamel sauce and preparing finely chopped onion!

If you master the art of preparing an onion professionally you will greatly enhance the speed at which you can work in the kitchen.

To chop or finely chop an onion, use the following method : **using a very sharp knife will save a lot of tears!** It is the vapour released by the onion which causes eyes to water and a blunt knife forces more vapour to escape.

❑ Cut off the top and root end of your onion, slice in two from top to bottom and remove the two outer skins.

❑ Lay one onion half, cut side down on your chopping board. With your knife pointing towards the root end, make parallel cuts, slicing downwards onto the board, to within about 1cm (¹/₂″) of the root end. **The more cuts you make, the smaller will be the pieces of onion.**

❑ Now slice down again, at right angles to the first cuts, and you will have small dice. **The thinner the slices, the smaller the dice.**

CARROTS

Baby carrots only need to be scrubbed clean and have their tops removed before cooking.
Small to medium carrots peel and cut into rings.
Larger ones peel, divide into two or three across and then cut into sticks.
A **teaspoon of sugar** will sweeten old carrots.

❑ Cook for 10 to 15 minutes, depending on size.
❑ Drain, then add a little butter to the saucepan, and stir to coat the carrots.

Serve sprinkled with fresh chopped parsley. Or they may be glazed — see Carrots Vichy below.

CARROTS À LA VICHY

Here is a very simple way to achieve the taste of glazed 'Carrots à la Vichy', and my favourite way of serving them.

To serve 4, take 500gr /1lb of carrots.

❑ Prepare them in rings and cook as above.
❑ Drain though a colander.
❑ Return the saucepan to the heat with a knob of butter and 1 tablespoon of caster sugar, stir until dissolved **but not browned**.
❑ Add the carrots and turn them until coated.
❑ Season with freshly ground black pepper.
Serve sprinkled with fresh chopped parsley.

SWEDE

"Pour les vaches" said my Mother-in-Law, looking down her very French nose! Indeed, in France swede is generally considered only fit for cattle. But small, young swede, properly prepared, is an excellent, contrasting second vegetable, especially with roast beef or steak and kidney pudding. Swedes are best early in the winter before they become fibrous. Choose small ones. Swedes have quite a thick skin, so use a small, sharp knife to cut off all the blemishes and skin.

❏ Cut the orange flesh into small cubes and cook for about 20 to 25 minutes, until tender.

❏ Drain and add a generous knob of butter, then mash with a potato masher and season with freshly milled black or white pepper.

MASHED SWEDE AND CARROT

This is a very sweet alternative to plain swede.

❏ Cook together equal quantities of swede and carrot, then mash together with a generous knob of butter, or a little cream, and season with freshly milled black pepper to serve.

POTATOES

The potato is often maligned. It is thought to be starchy and fattening but, weight for weight, bread contains $2\frac{1}{2}$ times as much carbohydrate as potato! Potato is rich in potassium and vitamin C and, being alkaline is very easily digested. It is a valuable part of a good, balanced diet.

There are literally dozens of ways of cooking potatoes, so here I have picked a few of my own favourites.

PLAIN BOILED POTATOES

New potatoes are delicious with sauce dishes, casseroles, pies, roasts, fish and salads. Small new potatoes only need to be washed before cooking.

❏ Cook for 15 to 20 minutes. A sprig of mint can be added to the cooking water to give a pleasant aromatic flavour.

❏ Serve, tossed in melted butter and sprinkled with fresh chopped parsley.

Old or 'Main Crop' potatoes need to be peeled and the larger ones cut, so that they are all of fairly equal size. Plain boiled potatoes go well with rich sauce dishes, casseroles, pies and fish.

❏ Cook for 25 to 30 minutes.

MASHED OR CREAMED POTATOES

Mashed potato is particularly good with all casseroles, boiled gammon, sausages, pork chops and steak and kidney pudding.

To produce light, fluffy mashed potatoes, you need old potatoes, cooked as for plain boiled. You will need about 1k /2lb for 4 people.

❏ When cooked place in a bowl. Use a masher (or potato ricer if you have one), to thoroughly mash until free from lumps.

❏ Return your saucepan to the stove and bring $\frac{1}{2}$ a cup of milk, with a generous knob of butter, to

the boil.
- ❏ As the milk and butter rise in the pan, quickly add the mashed potato and stir vigorously with a **wooden spoon**. (This gives a much lighter texture than a fork!) Season with freshly milled black pepper.

SAUTÉ POTATOES

Sauté potatoes go well with all grilled meats and fish. To be strictly correct, you should boil the potatoes in their skins and peel when cold. However, you can more easily use 'leftovers!' Clarified butter (see p.26) should also be used for frying, **as it will not burn**, but butter and oil together is perfectly satisfactory. **The oil helps to prevent the butter from burning.**

- ❏ Slice the potatoes evenly, fairly thin.
- ❏ Melt enough clarified butter, or unsalted butter with a little mild olive oil, in a frying pan to coat the potatoes. Season with salt and freshly ground pepper.
- ❏ **Place a lid on the pan** and cook over a medium heat for 3 to 5 minutes. **This will give a crisper result**.
- 4. Remove the lid and turn the potatoes, then continue to cook, without the lid, for a further 3 to 4 minutes, until golden brown.

The result should be free from surplus fat. Serve sprinkled with fresh chopped parsley.

ROAST POTATOES

Old or main crop potatoes are best. You will not get a really crisp result early in the season. Allow $1^1/_2$ to 2 potatoes per person.

Your oven will probably already be hot if you are roasting meat, but otherwise preheat it to 220°C/Gas Mark 7.

- ❏ Peel the potatoes and cut them to a uniform size.
- ❏ Boil for 10 minutes, then drain.

WHILE THE POTATOES ARE BOILING: heat up a couple of knobs of dripping or butter in your roasting dish.

- ❏ Put the potatoes into the roasting dish and turn them in the fat, seasoning with salt and freshly ground black pepper.
- ❏ Cook for 1 to $1^1/_2$ hours in the hot oven until golden brown and crisp.

PARSNIPS

When I was a boy parsnips came in many shape and sizes, but our clever farmers can now produce them straight and of uniform size! This certainly makes them easier to prepare.

- ❏ Peel and cut off any brown bits, then slice in half across. Cut the lower half in two lengthwise and the thicker half into similar sized sticks.
- ❏ Cook for 10 to 15 minutes.
- ❏ Test with a pointed knife. They should be tender but firm.
- ❏ Drain, then toss in melted butter and season with freshly milled black pepper to serve.

Parsnips are often roasted around a joint of beef but,

although crisp, they tend to be dry. When serving with roast beef, therefore, I prefer to boil them as above, allow to cool and then fry in butter or beef dripping.

PURÉE OF PARSNIPS & CARROTS

My father-in-law did not like either parsnips or carrots. One day, not knowing this, I cooked a purée of both! To his surprise, he enjoyed it enormously and is now an enthusiastic convert to this sweet and very easy dish!

❏ Cook equal quantities of parsnips and carrots together until soft.

❏ Pass them though a sieve or food processor.

❏ Add a little cream and freshly milled black pepper, blend in and serve.

RICE

I find, talking to a large number of cooks, that many have difficulty in cooking rice. Some have given up! Others use 'easy cook' varieties. The latter have good texture, but lack flavour. My personal choice for both taste and texture is basmati.

It really is not that difficult! Try this method for perfect fluffy rice — every time!

START COOKING YOUR RICE IN PLENTY OF TIME, or prepare it in advance and reheat when you are preparing your meal. Rice retains a lot of moisture so, after cooking , **it needs plenty of time to drain**.

TO SERVE 4 YOU WILL NEED:
250gr /8oz Rice
Water
Salt
A Little Butter

METHOD

1 Fill a large saucepan with cold, salted water, pour in the rice, stir well and bring to the boil, **without a lid**, on a medium heat.

2 Stir a couple of times and adjust the heat to keep the rice boiling steadily for 8 to 10 minutes. With a spoon, remove any scum.

3 Remove a little rice in a spoon and test a grain between your front teeth. When the texture is firm, but not hard, the rice is cooked.

4 Strain into a colander with small holes or a sieve and wash under a running cold tap. Allow to drain thoroughly for 5 to 10 minutes, shaking it occasionally.

TO REHEAT

Preheat the oven to 180°C/Gas Mark 4.

Butter a dish, place the rice in the dish, cover and reheat in the oven for 15 to 20 minutes. Or this can be done carefully in the microwave. **Take great care not to over-microwave**, or the result will be a nasty, sticky mess!

Rice will keep hot, well covered, until needed.

RATATOUILLE

See illustration p.148. This dish from Provence has a strong and distinctive taste, evoking the sunny climate from which it comes.

There are many variations, some cooking the vegetables separately and some without wine or garlic, but in one well-known establishment a young commis was sacked by the chef for forgetting to add garlic to the ratatouille — it is that important! **Cooking the vegetables together avoids an oily result**. In my opinion, the wine, too, plays an important part in the overall flavour and this recipe is, I think, the best.

Serve it hot as a vegetable, cold as a salad or part of an hors d'oeuvre. Placed in an ovenproof dish, sprinkled with cheese and browned under the grill it is also a good supper dish.

Ratatouille is an excellent accompaniment to steaks and grills, but is better not served with delicate dishes, which it would overwhelm.

It is difficult to make ratatouille economically for 2 or 4 people, because of the size of aubergines, I therefore usually make enough to use one aubergine and freeze what I do not need. It freezes and reheats extremely well.

A Chasseur casserole is the ideal pot to use.

TO SERVE 6 TO 8 YOU WILL NEED:

1 Medium Aubergine
*8 Medium Tomatoes**
        or 1x 800gr tin Italian tomatoes
1 Red Pepper
1 Green Pepper
4 Small Courgettes
2 Medium Onions
2 Cloves of Garlic
Olive Oil
½ Tablespoon Tomato Puree
½ Tablespoon Herbes de Provence
⅓ Bottle of Dry White Wine
Salt
        **Sugar (if using fresh tomatoes)*

PREPARATION AND METHOD

1 Take the aubergine, cut off each end and cut into small chunks. Place in a colander and sprinkle liberally with salt. **The salt prevents the aubergine from going brown and also removes its bitter flavour**. Set on one side.

2 Slice the peppers in half from top to bottom and remove the core and seeds. If you bang each half, cut side down, on your board it will shake out any remaining loose seeds. Cut out the whitish pieces of inside skin, then cut into pieces the size of a thumbnail.

3 Cut a small cross in the skin of the base of each tomato and put them in a bowl. Cover with boiling water. Let them soak for 2 or 3 minutes and then drain into a sieve or colander and douse with cold water. Remove the skins and cut each into eight pieces.

4 Slice the courgettes, **discarding the stem ends**, as these are bitter.

5 Skin the onions and cut into small cubes.

6 Crush the garlic.
7 Put the casserole onto a medium heat with a little olive oil and fry the onion and garlic until transparent but not brown.
8 Thoroughly wash the salted aubergine and add, together with the peppers, courgettes, tomatoes and tomato purée, to the onions and garlic in the pan. (**if you have used fresh tomatoes, add 2 teaspoons of sugar**). Sprinkle with the herbs, add the wine and bring to the boil.
9 Simmer, stirring from time to time, for 30 to 40 minutes, until tender.
   Check the seasoning before serving.

—ooOoo—

LYONNAISE POTATOES

This very tasty mix of onion and potato is delicious with roasts and grills and it keeps hot well. Very easy and quick. Illustration p.116 with lamb chops.

You can use leftover potatoes or, ALLOW ENOUGH TIME TO BOIL THE POTATOES AND ALLOW TO COOL.

TO SERVE 4 YOU WILL NEED:
5 or 6 Boiled Potatoes
1 Large Onion
Unsalted Butter
Mild Olive Oil

Salt & Freshly Milled Black Pepper
Fresh Chopped Parsley to Garnish

PREPARATION AND METHOD
Preheat your oven to 150°C/Gas Mark 2.
1 Slice the potatoes and set on one side.
2 Peel and slice the onions.
3 Heat a generous knob of unsalted butter and a little olive oil in a frying pan and cook the onion, with a lid on, for 2 to 3 minutes, turning from time to time. Remove when transparent and soft.
4 Place another knob of butter in the pan, add the potatoes and cook, with a lid on, for 2 to3 minutes.
5 Remove the lid, turn the potatoes, add the onions, season with salt and freshly milled black pepper and brown together.
6 Transfer to an ovenproof dish and place in preheated oven for 30 minutes.
To serve sprinkle with fresh chopped parsley.

DAUPHINOISE POTATOES

This is a deliciously subtle combination of potatoes and cheese. Baked in the oven, it makes a particularly good accompaniment to roast lamb and grills.

You can serve dauphinoise potatoes, as in France, as a separate course. It is also substantial enough to serve on its own as a light supper dish.

TO SERVE 4 YOU WILL NEED:
750gr /1¹/₂lb Old Potatoes
125gr /4oz Gruyere Cheese
450ml /³/₄ pint Milk
1 Clove of Garlic
Nutmeg (preferably freshly grated from whole nutmeg)
Unsalted Butter
Salt & Freshly Ground Black Pepper

PREPARATION AND METHOD
Preheat your oven to 190°C/Gas Mark 5.

1 Peel the potatoes and slice very thinly, using a sharp knife, mandolin slicer or food processor.
2 Grate the cheese.
3 Bring the milk to the boil.
4 Peel the garlic clove, cut it in half and rub it around to coat the inside surface of an ovenproof baking dish.
5 Melt a little butter and, using a pastry brush, paint the inside surface of the baking dish.
6 Place the potato, cheese and hot milk into a mixing bowl and season with salt and pepper, sprinkle with grated nutmeg and mix thoroughly.
7 Pour the mixture into the baking dish and scatter small pieces of butter on top.
8 Cook in **the centre** of your preheated oven for 45 minutes to 1 hour.

—ooOoo—

BUBBLE AND SQUEAK

Bubble and squeak is a wonderful accompaniment to all grills and cold meats. It is a delicious and economical using-up dish and one of my favourites.

I have had it with bacon fat to bind the potato and cabbage. The result, though tasty, was horribly indigestible! I use an egg and I feel sure you will find this recipe both tasty and digestible!

Although usually made with potatoes and cabbage, bubble and squeak is extremely good with any green leaf vegetable. The addition of a few cooked carrots or even green beans is delicious, so you can be creative and very economical with leftovers!

YOU WILL NEED:
Cooked Potatoes
Cooked Green Vegetables or Mixture of Vegetables
1 Egg
Unsalted Butter
Mild Olive Oil
Salt & Freshly Milled Black Pepper
Plain Flour (if making small cakes)

PREPARATION AND METHOD
1 Taking about half potato and half vegetable, mash these together and season well with salt and freshly ground black pepper. Add an egg and mix well with a wooden spoon.
2 Either leave to cook in one piece, or form into cakes with your hands and dust with flour.
3 Heat a frying pan on a medium to high heat, add a knob of butter and a little olive oil and fry the bubble and squeak until golden brown.If you are serving bubble and squeak for breakfast, it can be fried in the bacon fat.

SALADS

—ooOoo—

Salads give scope for endless variety and they can be served with cold meals or hot, as a meal on their own, or as an extra course, as in France.

FRENCH-STYLE SALADS

These salads are simple to prepare and are an economical way of using up leftover vegetables. They are made from a combination of raw and cooked vegetables, kept separate, but served together.

The secret is in the dressing. This should be delicate in flavour. For the French salads, and for all the salads in this chapter, the French dressing used is given on p.20 . Where mayonnaise is used, the recipe is given on p.22.

French salads can be eaten with cold meats, pies or quiches or used as part of an hors d'oeuvre.

Almost any combination can be put together, so you can be creative and guided by what you have available.

I have not specified quantities, as these will depend on how many people you are serving and how many different salads you make.

FRENCH GRATED CARROT SALAD

This sweet and delicate salad enhances any salad combination or plate of hors d'oeuvre and is very quick and easy.

YOU WILL NEED:
Raw Carrots
Caster Sugar
French Dressing
Salt & Freshly Milled Black Pepper

PREPARATION
❏ Peel and grate the raw carrots.
❏ Place in a bowl and sprinkle with caster sugar, a little salt and freshly milled black pepper and stir thoroughly.
❏ Add a little **well shaken** French dressing and stir again.

FRENCH TOMATO SALAD

This versatile salad can be used on its own, together with other French salads, or as a starter.

YOU WILL NEED:
Tomatoes
Onion
French Dressing (see p.20)
Salt & Freshly Milled Black Pepper
Fresh Chopped Parsley to Garnish

PREPARATION
- ❑ Using a sharp knife, **finely** chop an onion, or part of an onion, depending on how much salad you are making (see method for preparing an onion p.50.). The amount you use will depend on taste.
- ❑ Slice the tomatoes into 5 or 6 thin slices, discarding the top slice.
- ❑ Cover the base of a serving dish with sliced tomatoes, sprinkle with onion, season with a little salt and freshly ground black pepper. **Shake the French dressing well** to mix and sprinkle over the tomato and onion. Repeat, dressing and seasoning each layer.

TO SERVE : sprinkle with fresh chopped parsley.

FRENCH POTATO SALAD

You can use either French dressing or mayonnaise to dress potato salad. Preparation is the same for both but, if possible, use warm potatoes when using French dressing. A variation is to omit the onion and add finely chopped fresh chives.

YOU WILL NEED:
Cooked Potatoes (see p.51)
Onion
French Dressing (see p.20) **or** *Mayonnaise (see p.22)*
Salt & Freshly Milled Black Pepper
Cayenne Pepper to Garnish (optional)

PREPARATION
- ❑ Skin and finely chop some onion.
- ❑ Dice the cooked potatoes into a bowl and sprinkle with a little onion.
- ❑ Add well shaken French dressing or mayonnaise, season with a little salt and freshly ground black pepper and turn to coat the potato.

TO SERVE: Finish with chopped parsley or a sprinkle of cayenne pepper.

FRENCH LEEK SALAD

So simple!

YOU WILL NEED:
Cooked Leeks (see p.46)
French Dressing (see p.20)
Salt & Freshly Milled Black Pepper

PREPARATION
- ❏ Cut the leeks into pieces approx. 2.5 cm (1") to 5cm (2") in length.
- ❏ Place in a bowl, sprinkle liberally with **well shaken** French dressing, season to taste and stir to coat.

FRENCH GREEN BEAN SALAD

Another easy one!

YOU WILL NEED:
Cooked Green Beans (see p.46)
French Dressing (see p.20)
Salt & Freshly Milled Black Pepper

- ❏ Put the cooked beans in a bowl, season lightly with salt and freshly milled black pepper. Sprinkle with **well shaken** French Dressing, and stir to coat.

FRENCH CAULIFLOWER SALAD

Use **lightly** cooked cauliflower for this salad, **which is best made while still warm**.

YOU WILL NEED:
Cooked Cauliflower (see p.43)
French Dressing (see p.20)
Salt & Freshly Milled Black Pepper
Fresh Chopped Parsley

- ❏ Cut the cauliflower into small florets.
- ❏ Place in a bowl, season lightly with salt and freshly milled black pepper and sprinkle with **well shaken** French dressing. Turn to coat and sprinkle with chopped parsley.

FRENCH CELERIAC SALAD

This very 'French' salad is one found in almost all Charcuteries, but very easy to make yourself.

YOU WILL NEED:
Celeriac
Mayonnaise (see p.22)
Salt & Freshly Milled Black Pepper

PREPARATION
- ❏ Celariac has a thick outer skin which must be removed. Cut into pieces and grate into a bowl. Or you can use the julienne slicer disc on a food processor or a mandolin.
- ❏ Season lightly with salt and freshly milled black pepper. Add mayonnaise and stir to coat.

TOMATO AND AVOCADO SALAD

This is a substantial salad and can be served with cold meats etc., as a course on its own, a starter or a light supper dish. When serving for supper or a light snack, it is very good sprinkled with freshly grated parmesan, gruyere or cheddar cheese.

Allow about half an avocado per person and an equal amount of tomato.

YOU WILL NEED:

Tomatoes
Avocados
French Dressing (see p.20)
Salt & Freshly Milled Black Pepper

PREPARATION

❏ Slice the tomatoes into 5 or 6 thin slices, discarding the top slice.
❏ Halve, stone, peel and slice the avocado.
❏ Arrange the tomato and avocado in layers in a shallow dish. Season each layer lightly with salt and freshly milled black pepper and a liberal sprinkling of **well shaken** French dressing.

—ooOoo—

GREEN SALAD

One comes across many variations of green salad, including some with ingredients which are not all green! The traditional French green salad is simply lettuce, lightly coated in a mild dressing, with a faint hint of garlic. It is simple, light and refreshing and perfect to follow a steak or fish. Good too with cold meats, pies and quiches.

YOU WILL NEED:

Lettuce or Mixed Salad Leaves
Clove of Garlic
French Dressing (see p.20)
Salt & Freshly Milled Black Pepper

PREPARATION

❏ Wash the lettuce and spin to dry, then tear the leaves into manageable size.
❏ Cut a clove of garlic and rub it around a salad bowl, leaving a film of juice.
❏ **Shake the French dressing well** and put enough to coat the lettuce into the bowl.
❏ Add the lettuce, lightly season with salt and freshly milled black pepper, then gently turn and toss until lightly coated.

Do not toss your salad until you are ready to serve it or it will spoil.

—ooOoo—

LETTUCE AND EGG SALAD

This salad is typically French in its simplicity and can be served as an accompaniment to cold meats, pies and quiches, or as a separate course.

You can use any lettuce or, if you prefer, mixed salad leaves. Allow about half an egg per person.

YOU WILL NEED:

Lettuce or Mixed Salad Leaves
Eggs
French Dressing (see p.20)
Salt & Freshly Milled Black Pepper

PREPARATION

❑ To hard boil the eggs, bring a pan of water to the boil and add salt. Remove from the heat and gently lower the eggs into the pan. Return to the heat and boil for **10 minutes only. Douse in cold water and leave under a running tap until cold**. This will prevent that unpleasant grey rim round the yolk which is caused by overcooking.

❑ Wash and thoroughly drain the lettuce. Tear into medium sized pieces.

❑ Shell and cut the eggs into quarters.

When ready to serve, place the lettuce and eggs in your salad bowl, season with a little salt and freshly ground black pepper and add enough **well shaken** French dressing to coat. Turn the salad carefully to thoroughly mix.

Do not toss the salad until ready to serve as, once dressed, it will not keep.

COLESLAW

Made and eaten fresh, this is a crisp and refreshing salad. The bought variety often has been made with a sharp mayonnaise dressing and is sad in texture. Try this recipe, dressed with French Dressing.

TO SERVE 4 YOU WILL NEED:

$^1/_2$ *Small White Cabbage*
$^1/_2$ *Medium Onion*
2 Carrots
French Dressing (see p.20)
Salt & Freshly Milled Black Pepper

PREPARATION

❑ Skin and finely chop the onion.

❑ Peel and grate the carrots.

❑ Cut away the outer leaves of the cabbage, quarter and remove the hard core. Finely shred the quarters.

❑ Put all the prepared ingredients into a large bowl and mix together, adding salt and freshly milled black pepper. Sprinkle with **well shaken** French Dressing and mix well.

SALADE NIÇOISE

On a summer's day one of the most delightfully refreshing meals to enjoy 'al fresco' is a Salade Niçoise. For me it conjures up a beach café in Nice, a bottle of nicely chilled Provence Rosé, the smell of mimosa and the deep azure of the Mediterranean.

I have experienced a number of variations and the ingredients can vary according to availability, but the style of the dish should not. To set it out on a plate like an hors d'oeuvre, as so often done, is to miss the whole point of the dish!

I normally use either iceberg lettuce or little gem, but you may prefer to use mixed salad leaves.

TO SERVE 4 YOU WILL NEED:

Lettuce
1/2 a Small Onion
4 Medium Tomatoes
1/4 Cucumber
2 Sticks of Celery
Handful of Cooked Dwarf/Kenya Beans
1/2 Red Pepper
4 Hard Boiled Eggs
2 x 200gr Tins of Tuna Fish
1 Small Tin of Anchovies
Approx. 20 Ripe Black Olives
French Dressing (see p.20)
Salt & Freshly Milled Black Pepper

PREPARATION

❑ Hard boil the eggs. To avoid a black ring around the yolk, bring a pan of water to the boil and add salt. Remove from the heat and gently lower the eggs into the pan. Return to the heat and boil for **10 minutes only. Douse in cold water and leave under a running tap until cold.**

❑ Top and tail the beans and cut them in half. Cook in a pan of salted, boiling water, **without a lid**, for 4 to 5 minutes. Run under a cold tap in a sieve or colander to refresh and retain the colour. Set aside.

TO ASSEMBLE THE SALAD

1. Wash and dry the lettuce and tear into pieces.
2. **Finely** dice the onion (for method see p.50)
3. Cut the tomatoes in half and each half into 3 or 4.
4. Thinly slice the cucumber.
5. Trim and chop the celery into small chunks.
6. Core the red pepper and remove the pips. Cut into pieces to match the size of the celery.
7. Place all these ingredients into a bowl with the cooked beans and half the olives.
8. Drain the oil from the tin of tuna and add the tuna to the salad in chunks.

JUST BEFORE SERVING

1. Having **vigorously shaken the dressing**, sprinkle it over the salad and carefully turn to coat with the dressing.
2. Cut the eggs lengthways into quarters.
3. Decorate the top of the salad with the egg, anchovies and the rest of the black olives.

WARM SEAFOOD SALAD

This was a particularly popular dish in my restaurants. Rather expensive and time-consuming to produce, but well worth it.

The choice of fish can vary according to availability and personal taste, but I usually use lemon sole, salmon, scampi and prawns, which give a good variety of flavours.

This salad looks its most attractive served on individual plates.

ALLOW ENOUGH TIME TO THAW THE SCAMPI OR SCALLOPS AND PRAWNS. You can do this at room temperature, according to the instructions on the packet. However, I favour **thawing quickly to retain more of the juices**. To do this, remove the shellfish from their packet and place in **tepid** (not hot) water for about 20 minutes. If you use this method, you should use them immediately. **Do not thaw and then delay cooking**.

TO SERVE 4 YOU WILL NEED:
4 x 155gr /5oz Fillets of Fish
375gr /12oz **Unbreaded** *Scampi*
or *12* **Unbreaded** *Scallops*
250gr /8oz Peeled Prawns
Plain Flour
Unsalted Butter
Mild Olive Oil
French Dressing (see p.20)
Lettuce or Mixed Salad Leaves
Celery
Tomatoes
Cucumber
Salt & Freshly Milled Black Pepper
Fresh Chopped Parsley to Garnish

PREPARATION
- ❏ Thaw the scampi or scallops and prawns, if frozen, see above.
- ❏ Arrange a bed of lettuce or mixed salad leaves in the centre of each plate. Add a little chopped celery and surround with sliced cucumber and tomato.
- ❏ Skin the fish fillets (see p.82) and cut into bite-sized pieces.
- ❏ Put some flour on a plate, season it with salt and pepper and turn the fish and scampi (or scallops) in the flour to coat all over.

METHOD
1. Heat a knob of butter and a little oil in a frying pan over a high heat. When sizzling, put in the fish pieces and scampi or scallops and fry **quickly** for about 3 minutes, until golden brown. Season with salt and freshly ground black pepper. Add the prawns and allow to heat through.
2. Taking the fish, scampi and prawns from the pan with a slotted spoon or fish slice, arrange them on the salad bases.
4. Generously sprinkle each salad with **well shaken** French dressing and garnish with fresh chopped parsley.

SERVE IMMEDIATELY

SECRET OF SUCCESS: is to have an interesting mix of fish and seafood.

WARM KIDNEY AND BACON SALAD

The combination of tastes and textures in this salad is delightful! I only use **fresh** English lambs' kidneys, as imported or frozen kidneys tend to be strong and pappy.

Kidneys keep best if still in their fat but, in any case, use them as soon as possible.

TO SERVE 4 YOU WILL NEED:

8 English Lamb's Kidneys
8 Rashers of Bacon
2 Slices of White Bread
Unsalted Butter
Mild Olive Oil
French Dressing (see p.20)
Lettuce or Mixed Leaves
Celery
Tomatoes
Cucumber
Salt & Freshly Milled Black Pepper
Fresh Chopped Parsley to Garnish

PREPARATION & METHOD

1. Arrange a bed of lettuce or mixed salad leaves on individual plates, with a little celery, surrounded with sliced tomato and cucumber.
2. Slice each kidney in half lengthways, being careful to cut down through the **middle** of the core.
3. Remove the outer membranous skin.
4. THEN REMOVE THE CORE: hold the core firmly uppermost. Press your knife down against the flesh of the kidney, pull the core and cut as deeply as possible to remove the gristly white branches with the core. **Unless you remove the core and skin of the kidneys, they will shrink up and become tough when cooked**.
5. Slice each kidney half into three.
6. Remove the crusts from the bread and cut into small square croutons.
7. Remove the bacon rind.
8. Grill or fry the bacon until crispy, set aside and keep hot.
9. Place a generous knob of butter and twice as much oil in a frying pan on a medium/high heat. When sizzling hot, fry the croutons, turning them with a spoon until golden brown. Lift them out to drain on kitchen paper and keep hot.
10. Wipe out your frying pan with kitchen paper to remove any bread crumbs. Add a knob of butter and a little oil.
11. Sauté the kidney pieces over a high heat, turning them as they brown, for about 2 to 3 minutes. Season them while cooking in the pan with a little salt and black pepper. **Do not overcook**.
12. Cut the bacon into bite size pieces and scatter the bacon, kidney and croutons onto the salad bases.
13. Sprinkle well shaken French dressing generously over each salad, garnish with fresh chopped parsley.

SERVE IMMEDIATELY.

SECRET OF SUCCESS: is to prepare the kidneys well, so that they do not shrink and toughen when cooked.

STARTERS, HORS D'OEUVRE & PATÉ MAKING

introduction, suggestions, methods, techniques,
including flaming, and recipes

STARTERS

A starter should be an appetiser and a complement for what is to follow. A fish starter is a good prelude to a meat course and a paté, assiette de charcuterie, hors d'oeuvre or soup comes well before fish. You will find soups in Section 4.

When entertaining, if you choose a starter that needs little or no preparation or can be prepared in advance, you will have more time to prepare and cook the main course. If you are serving a cold meal or casserole, than you can devote more time to a starter.

Asparagus (p.49) and globe artichokes (p.49) are wonderful starters in season, as are avocado pears, either on their own, with French dressing set in the well, or as a salad with tomato (p.60). To select avocados, they must feel slightly soft to the touch at the stalk end. The smaller, thick, rough skinned variety cannot be felt in this way, they are ready to eat when the skin turns black. With avocados it is a good idea to buy them a day or two before needed. They can then, if necessary, be brought on in a warm place.

Melons are another good option. They are sometimes a bit difficult to select in good condition. To choose a melon, taking care not to bruise it, gently press the end opposite the stalk and, holding it to your nose, smell. If it is ready it will give off an aroma which will set your mouth watering!

Smoked salmon needs no preparation. Packets of ready sliced smoked salmon are adequate, but if you can buy it carved freshly from the side, you will appreciate a difference in taste, texture and quality. Spread the slices on individual plates, set a wedge of lemon on each plate and serve with thinly sliced brown bread and butter.Have black pepper or cayenne on the table.

Smoked trout, very like smoked salmon, is served in the same way. Also excellent are smoked trout fillets and whole smoked trout, which should be garnished with a wedge of lemon and a sprig of parsley and served with thin brown bread and butter and horseradish sauce.

Many recipes can be adapted to use for starters. For instance, Moules à la Marinière (p101), Scampi Provençale (p.102) and Scampi Meunière (p.103), Grilled Sardines (p.85), Sprats in White Wine (p95), Soused Herrings (p.96), Mackerel Poached in White Wine (p.94). All that is necessary is to reduce the quantities in the main recipes.

Tomato Salad (p.58) is a refreshing change, or a small Salade Niçoise (p.62).

Hors d'oeuvres have almost been forgotten, but this is such a pity, as they are so varied and so easy to prepare that I have devoted some space to the subject.

—ooOoo—

HORS D'OEUVRE

In my travels over the years I have come across many different presentations of hors d'oeuvre. It used to be a fashionable starter and most dining rooms and restaurants had an hors d'oeuvre trolley. In northern France a tray full of seafood would be brought to the table. There would be a glistening selection of crab, langoustines, prawns, shrimps, oysters, winkles, baby scallops etc. Having demolished that, there followed an equally large tray of charcuterie made up of paté, brawn, saucisson, different hams etc. And then the main course! How we ever managed cheese and dessert, as we sometimes did, I cannot now imagine!

The largest spread of hors d'oeuvre I was offered was in Valberg. A massive carved table, with pristine white damask cloth, was laden with dozens of tempting dishes from which you helped yourself.

More modestly, in Paris, 'Auntie' used regularly to have a simple hors d'oeuvre as a starter, particularly at lunchtime. This was an economical way of using up yesterday's leftover vegetables, meat or fish.

A good hors d'oeuvre as a starter or appetiser should comprise a small selection of contrasting savoury dishes and will depend on your own choice and what you have available. Ideally there will be some fish or meat, or both, and some vegetables.

Larger portions of hors d'oeuvre make an excellent light lunch or supper, particularly appealing for eating 'al fresco', accompanied by fresh crusty bread and modest wine!

I give below some suggestions from which you can make a selection. Quite a few are bought ready to serve, making hors d'oeuvre an easy option for a trouble free meal.

Recipes included in this book

Tomato Salad - p.58	Potato Salad - p.58
Carrot Salad - p.57	Leek Salad - p.59
Green Bean Salad - p.59	Cauliflower Salad - p.59
Celeriac - p.59	French Country Paté - p.68
Duck Terrine - p.69	Brawn Parisienne - p.75
Salmon Mayonnaise - p.91	
Prawns in Seafood sauce - p.100	
Crab in Seafood sauce - p.99	
Soused Herring - p.96	
Mackerel in White Wine - p.94	

To buy ready prepared

Ham
Parma Ham
Garlic Sausage
Salami
Smoked Trout
Smoked Mackerel
Smoked Herring
Smoked Sprats
Smoked Eel
Smoked Salmon

PATÉ MAKING

Strictly speaking a paté is cooked in pastry, and a terrine in a dish, but nowadays the distinction is rarely made and paté can be made, as I do, by cooking it in a bacon lined cast iron terrine or casserole.

In the past every French charcuterie made several patés, including its own 'Paté de Maison'. This was usually in a large, old, probably chipped, earthenware dish and could always be relied upon to be good. Sadly, the day of the bought-in, manufactured paté has arrived and made such delights almost a thing of the past. However, you can redress this loss by making your own!

Patés and terrines take a bit of forward planning to make because they need to marinate, but the actual preparation time is not long. Once made, they are a wonderful standby, as they keep well. Ideal for informal lunches or suppers with salad or fresh bread and butter, for a starter or for part of an hors d'oeuvre.

In this book I have given three recipes. The one for Duck Terrine can be varied by substituting chicken, pheasant or rabbit, using the same method and basic materials. Once the techniques for paté making are acquired there are plenty of recipes to try for variety. THE TECHNIQUE OF FLAMING IS WORTH ACQUIRING. It is used in making chicken liver paté and also in a number of casseroles and sauces. It is spectacular, but not difficult or dangerous if care is taken. However, I stress the importance of caution. **Take your time. Allow your pan to cool a little before pouring in the brandy or liqueur.** In this way the flames will not rise so high. **It is important to hold the pan at arms length** and to keep your head out of the way (eyebrows take a long time to grow). When ignited, either with a match or by tilting the pan towards the gas jet, the flames will shoot up, but soon die away. In some recipes the flames are quickly doused with liquid. Flaming burns off the alcohol and gives an enhanced, mellow flavour to the dish.

—ooOoo—

FRENCH COUNTRY PATÉ

This is a coarse, country paté, a real 'taste of France'. I usually prepare the ingredients and leave them to marinate overnight.
You will need a lidded terrine, Chasseur is ideal.

TO FILL A 1000ML /1³/₄ PINT TERRINE:
500gr /1lb Belly of Pork
125gr /4oz Chicken Livers
225gr /8oz Streaky Bacon cut thin
90gr /3oz Lard
1 Medium Onion
1 Carrot
1 Clove of Garlic
2 Teaspoons Whole Pickling Spice
Sprig of Fresh Parsley
2 Bay Leaves
1 Teaspoon Dried Thyme
2 Tablespoons Brandy
Approx. ¹/₄ Bottle of Red or White Wine
12gr /1 Tablespoon or 1 sachet Powdered Gelatine
Salt & Freshly Milled Black Pepper

PREPARATION & METHOD

1. Skin and trim gristle and bone from the pork and cut into cubes.
2. Peel the onion and carrot and cut into pieces.
3. Peel and finely chop the garlic.
4. Place the above ingredients in a bowl with the herbs and spices. Pour over the brandy and wine. Stir to mix all well together.

LEAVE TO MARINATE FOR 4 TO 6 HOURS OR OVERNIGHT.

TO ASSEMBLE THE PATÉ.

Preheat your oven to 180°C/Gas Mark 4.

1. Trim all the gristle from the chicken livers, taking **great care to remove any green pieces**. These are caused by the gall bladder, are very bitter and would spoil the paté.
2. Remove the rind and any gristle from the bacon and, on a board, using the flat of a cleaver or a wooden rolling pin, flatten enough rashers to line the inside of the paté terrine.
3. Remove the meat from the marinade. Strain off the liquid, discarding the vegetables and herbs and half the garlic. Set the liquid aside.
4. Mince the pork, liver and the rest of the bacon (retaining 2 rashers to top the paté) into a bowl.
5. Sprinkle the gelatine into the meats, season with salt and freshly ground black pepper and mix well.
6. Pour in the strained liquid, mix well together and put the mixture into the lined terrine. Cover with 2 rashers of streaky bacon.
7. Put the lid on the terrine. Place in a bain marie (a large dish containing enough water to reach about half way up the side of the terrine) and put in the preheated oven to cook for 1 hour.
8. Remove the lid and cook for a further $\frac{1}{2}$ hour.

To test, pierce the centre of the paté with a skewer or similar utensil, and press down. If clear liquid bubbles out it is cooked. If the liquid is cloudy, cook for a further 10 minutes and test again.

The liquid surrounding the paté after cooking forms a delicious jelly and helps to preserve it — don't be tempted to pour it away, as it is an integral part of the dish.

Cool at room temperature, covered with several layers of aluminium foil with a weight on top to compress the paté. Then chill well in the refrigerator. Remove the strips of bacon and seal the top with melted lard.

—ooOoo—

DUCK TERRINE

This is a very attractive paté, with contrasting colours, tastes and textures.

I use Barbary, Gressingham or Debden ducks whenever possible because they are leaner and more tasty than some others, which tend to be very fatty.

You will need a terrine with a lid. (I use cast-iron Chasseur.)

TO FILL A 1000ML /1³/₄ PINT TERRINE YOU WILL NEED:

1 Duck
750gr /1¹/₂lb Belly of Pork
2 Slices Streaky Bacon
Unsalted Butter
90gr /3oz Lard
1 Carrot
1 Onion
1 Bay Leaf
Sprig of Parsley
Sprig of Thyme or ¹/₂ tsp dried
75ml /3fl.oz Brandy
150ml /5fl.oz Stock
12gr /1 Tablespoon or 1 sachet Powdered Gelatine
Salt & Freshly Milled Black Pepper

PREPARATION & METHOD

1. Start by skinning the duck: run a sharp knife down the back and, using the knife where necessary, pull the skin away. It will not matter if the skin is in several pieces, but keep it as whole as possible.
2. Melt a small knob of butter and, using a pastry brush, paint the inside of your terrine, then line it with the duck skin (skin side out) and set aside.
3. Remove all the flesh from the duck and place in a bowl.
4. Peel and slice the carrot and onion and add to the duck, together with the herbs and brandy. Season well with salt and pepper and stir to mix well .
5. Press the mixture down and cover.

SET ASIDE TO MARINATE FOR 4 TO 6 HOURS.

6. Skin, bone and trim the pork and cut into large chunks.
7. Place the duck carcass, bones and trimmings, in a saucepan, cover with water and simmer, **without a lid**, for 1 hour.
8. Strain the liquid into a saucepan and boil, **without a lid**, until reduced by approximately half, to a well flavoured stock. Set aside. (Discard the carcass etc.)

TO ASSEMBLE THE TERRINE

Preheat your oven to 180°C/Gas Mark 4.

1. Heat 150ml/¹/₄ pint of the concentrated stock in a saucepan.
2. Slowly sprinkle the gelatine into the stock, stirring well until fully dissolved.
3. Remove the duck meat from the marinade. Sieve the liquid, discarding the vegetables and herbs, and set aside.
4. Slice six strips of breast meat, the thickness of your little finger, and set aside.
5. Add the remaining breast meat to the leg meat and pork. Place in a food processor with the

brandy and the gelatine, check the seasoning. Don't be too timid as paté needs to be well seasoned.

6. Into your lined terrine place a layer of the processed meats, then put 3 strips of breast on top and cover with more of the meat mixture. Add 3 more strips and fill the terrine with the remaining meat.
7. Cover the terrine with the streaky bacon.
8. Place the terrine, with its lid on, in a bain marie (a large dish containing enough water to reach about halfway up the side of the terrine) and cook in the preheated oven for 1 hour.
9. Remove the terrine lid and cook for a further ¹/₂ hour.

To test, pierce the centre of the paté with a skewer or similar utensil and press down. If clear liquid bubbles out, it is cooked. If the liquid is cloudy, cook for a further 10 minutes and test again.

The liquid surrounding the paté after cooking forms a delicious jelly and helps to preserve it.

Cool at room temperature, covered with several layers of aluminium foil with a weight on top to compress the paté. Chill thoroughly in the refrigerator. When chilled, remove the strips of bacon and seal the top with melted lard.

—ooOoo—

CHICKEN LIVER PATÉ

This is a smooth paté and very easy to make. The addition of Madeira wine and flaming sweetens and softens the flavour of the livers The technique of flaming is fully explained, on p.68.
Use a small terrine or mould for this paté.

TO SERVE 6 TO 8 STARTERS YOU WILL NEED:
250gr /¹/₂lb Chicken Livers
375gr /³/₄ lb Unsalted Butter
1 Small Onion
¹/₂ Clove of Garlic
¹/₂ Teaspoon Dried Thyme
150ml /4fl.oz Madeira Wine
75ml /2fl.oz Brandy
Salt & Freshly Milled Black Pepper
Melted Butter to Seal

PREPARATION
❏ Thoroughly trim the livers, removing any gristle. Be particularly careful to **cut away any green discoloration**. This is caused by the gall bladder and is very bitter. Occasionally you will find a gall bladder attached to a liver, it is about the size of a pea and blackish green in colour. **Be sure to discard it**.
❏ Skin and cut the onion into small chunks.
❏ Crush the garlic.

71

METHOD

1. Melt a large knob of butter in a frying pan and cook the onion and garlic over a medium heat until transparent. A lid on the pan will speed the process. Remove from the pan and set on one side.
2. Turn the heat to high. Add another knob of butter to the frying pan. When it is sizzling, put in the livers and fry quickly, turning them with a slice. **Do not cook through** (2 to 3 minutes only). Sprinkle them with thyme and then flame with brandy:- see p.68. Allow the flames to die down.
3. Now, mince the liver, onion and garlic together, or combine in a food processor.
4. Melt the remaining butter in a saucepan over slow to medium heat, add the minced ingredients and the Madeira wine. Season with salt and freshly ground black pepper. Simmer for 5 minutes, stirring from time to time.
5. Allow to cool for 5 minutes and then liquidise or process until smooth.
6. Pour into a suitably sized mould or terrine.
7. Chill thoroughly and, **when cold**, seal the top with melted butter.

SECRET OF SUCCESS: is not to overcook the livers.

—ooOoo—

Salade Niçoise
Recipe p.62

BRAWN

Do not be put off by commercially produced brawn, this old fashioned dish, when home-made, is as different as chalk from cheese! Traditionally, brawn is made from half a pig's head and a hock of bacon, but I have made many a bowl of brawn using a piece of shoulder or belly of pork instead of the half head and this is the recipe I recommend.

As the brawn needs to be chilled overnight in the fridge, MAKE IT THE DAY BEFORE REQUIRED.

TO FILL A 1000ML /1³/₄ PINT TERRINE OR SOUFFLE YOU WILL NEED:

750gr /1¹/₂lb Pork Belly or Shoulder
1 Hock of Bacon OR 375gr /12oz Piece of Shoulder Bacon
90gr /3oz Lard
1 Bay Leaf
Sprig Parsley
Sprig of Thyme or ¹/₂ tsp dried
¹/₂ Tablespoon Whole Pickling Spice tied in a sachet (see p.23) removing the red chillies
12gr /1 Tablespoon or 1 sachet Powdered Gelatine
Salt & Freshly Milled Black Pepper

PREPARATION & METHOD

1. Place the pork and bacon, spices and herbs in a large saucepan and cover well with water. Bring to the boil and **simmer gently with the lid on** for 3 hours.

Check from time to time and top up with water from a boiling kettle if necessary.

2. Allow to cool.
3. Strain off the liquid and set aside.
4. Trim all the meat from the bones, discarding bones, excess fat, skin and gristle.
5. Put all the trimmed meat on a large board and, with a large knife or cleaver, chop it fairly fine. Put into a bowl.
6. Heat 20fl.oz /1 pint of the saved liquid. Slowly sprinkle in the gelatine and mix well until thoroughly dissolved. Pour over the meats in the bowl and mix well together.
7. Test for seasoning and pour into a mould.

CHILL IN THE REFRIGERATOR OVERNIGHT.

8. Melt the lard and pour over the brawn to seal it. This will protect it from the air and preserve the brawn for up to a week in the fridge.

TO USE, keep the brawn in its mould and slice as required, covering the cut end with clingfilm to prevent it becoming dry.

SERVE brawn with salad and other cold meats, as a main meal, a starter or as part of an hors d'oeuvre. Or try the following Parisienne way of serving it.

—ooOoo—

BRAWN PARISIENNE

Served in this way many people who have wrinkled their noses at the thought of brawn, including my wife who was an avowed brawn hater, have been completely converted!

METHOD

1. Cut slices of brawn into pieces about the size of a postage stamp.
2. Sprinkle with finely chopped onion (see method p.50), French dressing (p.20) and fresh chopped parsley.

See illustration p.45

—ooOoo—

SMOKED SALMON PATÉ

With any paté, meat or fish, it is important to achieve a subtle blend of flavours. **Be particularly careful not to overdo the garlic** in smoked salmon paté, you only need a hint.

You can use smoked salmon trimmings, which will make this paté more economical, the pack may, however, contain some hard pieces, which you should discard.

This paté is very easy to make and, if you have a food processor or liquidiser, only takes about 20 minutes.

TO SERVE 4 TO 6 YOU WILL NEED:

100gr /4oz Smoked Salmon
200gr /6$\frac{1}{2}$ oz Philadelphia Cheese
50gr /2oz Unsalted Butter
50ml /2fl.oz Dry White Wine
$\frac{1}{4}$ Small Clove of Garlic
Juice of $\frac{1}{4}$ Lemon
Pinch of Cayenne Pepper

PREPARATION & METHOD

1. Soften the butter.
2. Cut the smoked salmon into small pieces.
3. Crush the garlic.
4. Place together in the food processor or liquidiser.
5. Give a quick spin, then add the wine, lemon juice and cayenne pepper. Spin until smooth.
6. Add the cheese in knobs and spin to blend thoroughly
7. Scoop the paté into a mould and chill.

SMOKED MACKEREL PATÉ

Use mackerel fillets and the same ingredients and quantities as for smoked salmon paté, above. Mackerel, however, will require more preparation:–
1. Remove the skin.
2. Trim off any hard pieces and be careful to remove any small bones.
3. Follow method and preparation as for Smoked Salmon paté .

75

Fresh Prawns with Mayonnaise
Recipe p.100

Moules à la Marinière   *Recipe p.101*

FISH & SHELLFISH
how to buy and prepare fish, grilling, frying,
poaching, sousing and recipes

FISH

My first taste of really fresh fish was as a young officer in the RNVR at the end of the last war aboard a minesweeping trawler in the North Sea. Following depth charge practice the call 'boats away' meant a scramble to retrieve dozens of fish thrown up by the explosions. The resulting meal was wonderful and depth charge practices were exceedingly popular! I have, ever since, had a particular love of fish and seafood.

To choose fresh fish, look for brightness. The skin should still be glistening with sea slime and a really fresh fish will be stiff. If the fish looks dull and limp, do not buy it.

If you have a good, reliable fishmonger in your area you are lucky, for there are not many left. Europe does better, they still have wonderful fresh fish markets on most days almost everywhere. A typical town in Normandy has ten or more bakers and butchers and a large, busy, prospering fishmonger. What a picture! A slab full of really fresh, glistening fish of every variety and a tank full of live crabs and lobsters.

Commercially frozen fish is a poor substitute for fresh. The process of freezing (particularly if the fish is not frozen the day it is caught) breaks down the tissue so that, when thawed, the juices drain out. You can overcome this, to a certain extent, by **thawing the fish quickly in tepid water**, then cooking it as soon as it is thawed, using a high heat to seal in the remaining juices.

If you freeze your own fresh fish you will get a better result. You need a quick-freezing compartment in your freezer. For whole sole, plaice, dab or flounder, **do not wash**, simply wrap each fish in clingfilm, for large fish cut into portions and wrap individually in clingfilm. **Herring and mackerel do not freeze well**.

The most common sin committed when cooking fish is overcooking. **Be very careful with timing, err on the side of undercooking**.

Also do not keep it hot for more than 15 minutes. Should this be necessary, simply cover with tin foil to keep the steam in. **Do not put in a hot cupboard or oven**.

Pan Fried Dover Sole Meunière
Recipe p.87

Mackerel Poached in
White Wine
Recipe p.94

PREPARATION OF RAW FISH

You will need a really sharp 6" filleting knife, kitchen scissors, a large chopping board and a piece of clean cloth.

A good fishmonger or supermarket will prepare your fish for you. If, on the other hand, you have the opportunity of buying really fresh fish from the coast or market, don't be daunted by the idea of preparing your own, you will be rewarded by a taste and freshness not normally available — mild, delicious and succulent!

Always take care, when washing, to remove all the blood around the backbone in the cavity, or it will give a bitter taste.

To fillet cod, whiting, mackerel and salmon :
1. Remove the head, cut off the fins with scissors and wash well under a running cold tap.
2. Lay the fish on a board with it its back facing you. Hold the head end, using a cloth.
3. Insert the knife, blade towards the tail, from a point just below the dorsal fin. With the knife following the backbone and sliding over it, slice down towards the tail, removing the flesh from the bones.
4. Turn the knife and slice from first incision up to the head near the backbone. Now lift the flesh and cut it away from the ribs.
5. Turn the fish over and repeat for the second fillet.

To fillet plaice or lemon sole:
1. Leave the skin on, cut off the head and remove the fins with scissors. Wash well under running cold water.
2. Using a cloth to hold the fish, lay it flat on a chopping board and run a sharp knife down the centre line, slicing through to the backbone.
3. Holding the knife nearly flat against the backbone, insert it in the middle and, following the backbone, remove the flesh from the bone, towards the tail and the fin edge. Turn the knife and repeat towards the head end.
4. Repeat to remove the flesh from the opposite side of the backbone.
5. Turn the fish over and repeat, to give four fillets.

WHEN GRILLING OR FRYING LEAVE THE SKIN ON, BUT FOR SAUCE DISHES IT IS BEST TO REMOVE THE SKIN.

To skin the fillets :
Insert the knife between the flesh and the skin at the tail end and cut a flap. With the fillet flat on the board skin side down, hold the flap, using a cloth to give grip. Insert the knife blade facing away from you, pull the skin and work the knife to and fro. It's really quite easy!
When serving small plaice and lemon sole whole, just cut off the head below the gills, cut off the fins and clean well under a running cold tap.

To skin Dover Sole

Wash well, removing any blood from the cavity. When served whole, leave the head on. Some cooks leave the white skin, but I prefer to remove both black and white skin :

1. Cut off the fins with scissors.
2. Start with the black side, using a cloth to hold the fish and grip the skin, make an incision just above the tail, insert the point of the knife and cut a flap of skin. Lift this flap and, holding it with the cloth, run your thumb under the skin to loosen it, about halfway up each side.
3. Gripping the fish in one hand and holding the skin with the cloth, pull the skin up towards the head. It should come away easily. If you become really skilled, you will be able to turn the skin over the head without breaking and run it down the other side to the tail. But, otherwise, simply repeat the process as for the black skin.

To de-scale Salmon

1. Trim off the fins with scissors.
2. Hold the fish by the tail and with a bluntish knife, held at a fairly acute angle, scrape the skin towards the head, removing the scales. Descaling is a messy business, but not difficult.

GRILLING FISH

Keep a separate tray or griddle for fish to save your grill pan from becoming fishy. Place it under the grill on top of the grill pan. This way, being nearer the grill, the fish will cook quicker.

Always light the grill and allow it time to reach maximum heat before starting to cook your fish. **Fish should be grilled quickly to seal and retain the juices and, therefore, flavour.**

Grilled fish is best served with a simple vegetable. New, plain boiled, or sauté potatoes, either on their own or with a fresh green vegetable — spinach, beans, peas or broccoli.

In the following instructions I have suggested the use of melted butter and a little oil (I usually use groundnut) but should you wish to reduce your butter consumption, use oil on its own and here I would advocate a top grade, mild, first cold pressing, olive oil. But the most important thing is that **it must be fresh.** Stale oil will give an unpleasant tang.

*Fillet of Lemon Sole
with Prawns and Mushrooms*
Recipe p.88

GRILLED WHOLE DOVER SOLE, PLAICE AND LEMON SOLE

METHOD

Turn on the grill and allow it come to full heat.

1. Melt a knob of unsalted butter and a little oil on the grilling tray and spread it all over.
2. On a plate, dust the fish with flour all over and season with salt and freshly ground black pepper.
3. Remove the tray from the grill, turn the fish in the melted butter and return to the grill, (plaice or lemon sole black skin uppermost) cook for 3 to 4 minutes.
4. Turn and cook for a further 3 minutes. Exact timing will depend on size and thickness.

TO TEST: insert a knife through to the backbone and lift a little flesh. If the bone is still pink, baste with a little butter or oil and cook for a further 2 minutes.

GRILLED SARDINES

Sardines will be sold unprepared, as they are small and very easy to clean. Just slit the underbelly, remove the gut and wash very thoroughly under cold running water. Leave the heads on.

Allow 2 or 3 sardines per person as a starter and 5 or 6 for a main course, depending on size.

METHOD

Heat the grill and allow it to reach full heat.

1. Melt a knob of unsalted butter and a little oil on a grilling tray and spread it all over.
2. On a plate, dust the sardines with flour all over and season with salt and freshly ground black pepper.
3. Remove the tray from the grill, turn them in the melted butter and return to the grill. Cook for 2 minutes.
4. Turn and cook for a further 2 minutes.

Simply serve with fresh bread and butter and garnish each helping with a lemon wedge and sprig of parsley.

GRILLED MACKEREL, HERRINGS AND TROUT

For herring and mackerel, take the prepared fish and make three diagonal cuts each side through to the backbone, to speed cooking. Trout are cooked whole without diagonal cuts.

METHOD

Heat the grill and allow it to reach full heat.

1. Place a large knob of unsalted butter and a little oil on a grill tray, to melt.
2. Using a pastry brush, paint the fish with the melted butter, season with salt and freshly milled black pepper and place back under the grill. Grill for 3 to 4 minutes.
3. Turn and cook for a further 4 minutes.

TO TEST mackerel and herring lift the flesh at the thick end with a knife and, if the backbone is still pink, baste with butter or oil and cook for a further 2 minutes.

TO TEST trout check inside the cavity that the backbone is not pink.

SERVE with a wedge of lemon and a sprig of fresh parsley to garnish.

—ooOoo—

GRILLED SALMON AND COD STEAKS OR CUTLETS

METHOD

Heat the grill and allow it to reach full heat.

1. Place a large knob of unsalted butter and a little oil on a grill tray, to melt.
2. Using a pastry brush, paint the fish with melted butter and sprinkle with a little flour.
3. Season with salt and freshly milled black pepper. Place under the grill for 3 to 4 minutes.
4. Turn and cook for a further 3 minutes.

TO TEST, dig the point of a knife into the centre of the round bone and, if it lifts out cleanly, the fish is cooked

TO SERVE: remove the bone and skin from each steak. Garnish with a wedge of lemon and a sprig of fresh parsley.

—ooOoo—

GRILLED FILLETS OF SALMON, COD, PLAICE AND LEMON SOLE

Fillets of all fish are grilled in the same way.

METHOD

Turn on the grill and allow to reach full heat.

1. Melt some unsalted butter and a little oil on your tray under the grill.
2. On a plate, dust the fillets lightly with flour.
3. Remove the tray from the grill, turn the fillets in the butter and lay them, skin side down. Season with salt and freshly milled black pepper and return to grill.

Do not turn the fillets over, only cook on one side. Timing will vary according to thickness.

❑ PLAICE AND LEMON SOLE fillets cook in approximately 4 to 5 minutes.

❑ COD AND SALMON will take from 6 to 8 minutes.
TO TEST: lift a flake. If not cooked baste with a little butter and cook for a further 2-3 minutes.

SERVE with a wedge of lemon and a sprig of fresh parsley to garnish.

—ooOoo—

PAN FRIED FISH

Preparation of the fish and cooking times are similar to grilling. Pan frying has the advantage of quickly sealing and retaining the fish juices. I use a Chasseur frying pan, which is designed for high heats.

As with grilling, you can use either butter with a little oil, or substitute a good, fresh, mild olive oil, but make sure your pan is sizzling hot before placing the floured fish in it.

You can serve the fish plain or with a lemon and butter dressing (Meunière).

—ooOoo—

PAN FRIED FILLETS OF SALMON, COD, PLAICE AND LEMON SOLE

METHOD
1. Lightly flour the fillets on both sides and season with salt and freshly milled black pepper.
2. Heat unsalted butter and oil in equal quantities to generously cover the base of a thick based frying pan, and place over a high heat. When sizzling, add the fish fillets, **flesh side down**, and cook for 2 to 3 minutes until golden brown.
3. Turn and cook for a further 2 to 3 minutes.

For thick cod fillets, allow more time and cover with a lid after the fish has been browned and turned.

SERVE plain, garnished with a wedge of lemon and sprig of fresh parsley, or 'meunière' (see p.103).

—ooOoo—

PAN FRIED WHOLE SMALL CODLING, WHITING, TROUT, DOVER SOLE, PLAICE AND LEMON SOLE

METHOD
1. Lightly flour the fish all over and season with salt and freshly ground black pepper.
2. Heat a knob of butter and an equal quantity of oil in a thick based frying pan over a high heat and, when sizzling, put in the fish. Cook for 3 to 4 minutes.
3. Turn and cook for another 3 to 4 minutes.

If the fish is thick, use a lid to help the cooking process after turning. Timing will vary according to size and thickness.

TO TEST, lift a little flesh at the thick end. If the backbone is still pink, continue to cook for a further minute or two with the lid on.

TO SERVE: codling, whiting and trout are best plain. Just garnish with a sprig of fresh parsley and wedge of lemon. Dover sole, plaice and lemon sole are best served either plain or "meuniere" (see p.103)

—ooOoo—

TROUT WITH ALMONDS

IN ADVANCE :

1. Take about 20gr ($^3/_4$ oz) of flaked almonds per portion and place on a tray or tin foil under a medium grill. Toast until just browned. **Do not turn your back, they cook very quickly and care needs to be taken to avoid burning.** Set on one side.

PREPARE AND PAN FRY THE TROUT AS ABOVE, cover with tin foil to keep warm then :

2. Melt about 30gr (1oz) per person of unsalted butter in a small saucepan, add the almonds and spoon over the cooked fish.

—ooOoo—

FILLET OF PLAICE OR LEMON SOLE WITH PRAWNS AND MUSHROOMS

This dish from Brittany is very pretty, topped with sliced mushrooms and pink prawns and a sprinkling of fresh green parsley(see illustration p.84). It is ideal for a special celebration meal, although it does mean the cook being absent at the last minute. However, if you have all your preparation done and your pans ready on the stove, it will take under 10 minutes to cook and serve. Leave your guests supplied with plenty of wine, good conversation will flow and they will hardly notice your absence!

TO SERVE 4 YOU WILL NEED:
4 Fillets of Plaice or Lemon Sole
Unsalted Butter
Mild Olive Oil
Plain Flour
<u>For the Sauce</u>
120gr /4oz Frozen Prawns
60gr /2oz White Mushrooms
Juice of $^1/_2$ Lemon
125gr/4oz Unsalted Butter
Freshly Chopped Parsley

ADVANCE PREPARATION

1. Allow the prawns to thaw at room temperature or, **if you are going to cook them straightaway**, thaw by placing in tepid water for about 10 minutes.
2. Put the butter for the sauce ready in a thick based saucepan.
3. Squeeze the lemon juice and set on one side.
4. Wash and slice the mushrooms.
5. On a plate, dust the fillets with flour on both sides and season with salt and freshly milled black pepper.

MAKE THE GARNISH
1. Heat a generous knob of butter in a saucepan and fry the mushrooms until just soft.
2. Add the prawns, heat through and keep warm.

DO NOT BOIL OR THE PRAWNS WILL SHRINK AND TOUGHEN

TO COOK THE FISH
1. Heat a generous knob of unsalted butter and a little oil in a thick based frying pan over a medium/high heat. When sizzling, add the fish fillets, flesh side down, and cook for 2 to 3 minutes until golden brown.
2. Turn and cook for a further 2 minutes.

TO SERVE
1. Put the fish onto hot plates or a serving dish.
2. Decorate each portion with some prawns and mushrooms.
3. Bring the butter to the boil and add the lemon juice.
4. As it froths in the pan, spoon over the cooked fish.
5. Garnish with a sprinkling of fresh chopped parsley.

—ooOoo—

POACHING

When I was a child recovering from illness I had to endure what we called a 'slops diet'. Beef tea, bread and milk and poached fish. The fish was cooked in either milk or water, without added seasoning and was horribly insipid. It put me off for years!

Fish poached in a court-bouillon (see p.90), however, is an altogether different 'kettle of fish'! Testimony to this is my experience when staying with friends in Scotland. I was, not unusually, pressed into service in the kitchen! It was summer, when nearly everyone responds to the warm evenings by serving poached salmon for their dinner parties. Unknown to me, my pal had had a surfeit, so when I, too, produced fresh salmon mayonnaise it was received with a distinct lack of enthusiasm! To my great surprise, however, he asked me a few days later if I would do it again!

The reason for this change of heart was that I had poached the salmon in a 'court-bouillon', an aromatic liquid produced from cooking together a mixture of vegetables, herbs and spices, which gives an enhanced and subtle flavour to the fish which cannot be achieved by plain poaching or cooking in foil in the oven. It takes only minutes to make and it is well worth those few minutes.

You will find a Chasseur shallow serving dish ideal for poaching fish.

COURT-BOUILLON

I use a **salty** court-bouillon with fish because, when poaching, it is in the water for only a few minutes and does not, therefore, absorb much salt. Which vegetables you use are not absolutely crucial so improvise if necessary with what you have available. Here is my recipe :

MAKES APPROX. 1150ML /2 PINTS YOU WILL NEED:

1 Large Carrot
1 Onion
½ Lemon
1 Bay Leaf
1 Sprig Thyme or ½ tsp dried
1 Sprig Parsley
1 Teaspoon Whole Pickling Spice
2 Tablespoons White Wine Vinegar
1 Tablespoon Salt
About 1500ml /2½ pints Water

PREPARATION & METHOD

1. **Discard any small pieces of red chilli from the pickling spice**.
2. Peel and chop the vegetables and place all the ingredients in a saucepan. Add the water and salt and boil until the vegetables are cooked (about 25 minutes).
3. Strain through a sieve and use the clear liquid for poaching your fish.

—ooOoo—

POACHED TROUT

Nothing can compare with trout straight from a mountain stream! When really fresh trout is cooked within an hour or two of being caught, it turns blue when poached and is then called Blue Trout.

Once, holidaying in Antibes, I spotted a trout tank in the supermarket. "Ah!" I thought "I must introduce my young daughters to Blue Trout". I made my purchase, went home and made a court-bouillon, then 'voila!' served Blue Trout. Oh, what a disappointment! They were inedible, tasting strongly of chlorine! We all have our failures!

Having bought your **fresh** trout, have a go, using a court-bouillon for enhanced flavour.

ALLOW ENOUGH TIME (ABOUT HALF AN HOUR) TO MAKE THE COURT-BOUILLON IN ADVANCE. As trout is a freshwater fish, **make sure that the court-bouillon is salty**.

PREPARATION
Wash the trout.

METHOD

1. Heat the court-bouillon in a pan deep enough for it to cover the fish.
2. When simmering, put in the fish and poach for 8 minutes. **Do not fast boil**.

SERVE simply garnished with a sprig of parsley and a wedge of lemon, or the addition of melted butter or Hollandaise Sauce (see p.25) is good too.

POACHED SALMON

What a change has taken place. Gone are the days when salmon was only available during the season and it was an expensive luxury. Now, with farmed salmon, it is available throughout the year and reasonably priced. Perhaps not to compare with wild salmon, but nonetheless a joy when well cooked.

 I have already dealt with grilled and fried salmon, but the best way to enjoy its delicate flavour is to poach it. This way it is enchanced by the subtle hint of herbs and spices from the court-bouillon. Cooked in this way you achieve maximum flavour and succulence, which is lost by baking.

If you are poaching a whole fish, you will need a fish kettle and enough court-bouillon (see p.90) to well cover the fish.

Wash and descale the salmon (see p.83) .

ALLOW ABOUT 30 MINUTES TO MAKE YOUR COURT BOUILLON IN ADVANCE.

METHOD

1. Put the salmon in the fish kettle, cover with court-bouillon and bring to the boil.
2. Reduce the heat to a **slow** simmer, leaving the lid on, and cook for 20 minutes.
3. Leave the fish in the water for a further 10 minutes, then lift out and place on a large oval serving dish.

TO SERVE HOT first remove all the fin bones and then carefully remove the skin. Garnish the dish with wedges of lemon and sprigs of parsley. It is especially good with an accompanying sauce such as hollandaise (see p.25) or caper (p.18).

TO SERVE COLD (for perfection just tepid) remove all the fin bones and then carefully remove the skin. Decorate the fish with slices of cucumber. Set lemon wedges and cucumber slices around the edge of the plate, then serve with fresh home-made mayonnaise (see p.22).

To portion the salmon, either hot or cold, using large fish servers, run the knife down the centre line, then fold back the flesh from the centre outwards, away from the ribs and the backbone and cut into portions. When the top half of the fish has been served, remove the tail, backbone, ribs and head and portion the remaining half.

POACHED SALMON STEAKS OR FILLETS

Although it is impressive to bring a whole hot garnished salmon to the table, skinning and serving it is quite difficult, therefore I would advise, except for a very special occasion or buffet, that you cook it in portions. Most salmon is sold in steaks or fillets and these are easy to deal with and quick to poach.

PREPARATION
Make enough court-bouillon (see p.90). Wash the pieces of salmon gently under cold running water.

METHOD
1. Choose a shallow pan, deep enough for the court-bouillon to cover the fish.
2. Bring to the boil, then reduce the heat to a **slow** simmer.
3. Place the fish in the pan and simmer gently for 6 to 8 minutes.
4. Leave the salmon, covered in the liquid for 2 to 3 minutes.
5. Lift out and drain.

TO SERVE: the fillets or steaks can be covered with foil to keep hot if serving with a sauce (see below) or set aside to cool.

POACHED SALMON WITH HOLLANDAISE SAUCE

Salmon with Hollandaise Sauce is one of the Classics, a really wonderful combination of taste and texture.

Make the sauce (see p.25) before poaching the salmon as above and serve hot.

—ooOoo—

POACHED SALMON WITH CAPER SAUCE

The piquancy of caper sauce complements salmon very well, it is rather easier to make than Hollandaise and therefore makes a useful alternative.

Make the sauce (see p.18) before poaching the salmon as above and serve hot.

—ooOoo—

SALMON MAYONNAISE

While the salmon is cooling, make a home-made mayonnaise (p.22). Serve this with the salmon before it is quite cold. The flavour of salmon is so much better if not chilled.

—ooOoo—

FILLET OF PLAICE OR SOLE 'À LA BONNE FEMME'

This is a special occasion dish with a lovely, mild combination of mushrooms and shallots in the sauce, which enhances but does not mask the fish. **In all fish cookery, it is important not to kill its delicacy**. If the accompanying sauce or garnish is too strong it will clash with the fish and spoil it.

When you buy your fish, have the fillets skinned and ask for the bones and **white** skin for a fish stock (black skin will discolour the stock), or remove the skin yourself (see p.82).

To really set this dish off, pipe mashed potato around the edge before adding the fish. Heat it under the grill and then return to the grill again with the fish, so that it browns. If you are going to do this, HAVE YOUR MASHED POTATO READY IN ADVANCE. But **make your mashed potato without any milk** or the milk will ooze out through your piping bag! Instead, use an egg and butter to blend the potato. Serve with runner, French beans or spinach.

IN ADVANCE

❑ Make 1150ml /2 pints of court-bouillon (see p.90)
❑ Boil and mash enough potato to surround your serving or individual dishes.

TO SERVE 4 YOU WILL NEED:

4 x Fillets (about 200gr each)
1150ml /2 pints Court-Bouillon (p.90)
Water
Mashed Potato (optional)

For the Sauce:

250gr /8oz Button Mushrooms
4 Shallots or ¹/₂ Medium Onion with ¹/₄ Clove of Garlic
150ml /¹/₄ pint Dry White Wine
600ml /1 pint Fish Stock
45gr /1¹/₂ oz Unsalted Butter
45gr /1¹/₂oz Plain Flour
2 Egg Yolks
Salt & Freshly Milled Black Pepper
Fresh Chopped Parsley to Garnish

PREPARATION

❑ Cover the fish bones and skin with water in a saucepan and boil for 30 minutes to make about 600ml/1 pint of stock, or use ¹/₂ chicken cube in 600ml/1 pint of water.
❑ Wash and slice the mushrooms.
❑ Skin and dice the shallots or onion finely (see p.50).

TO MAKE THE SAUCE

1. Melt the butter in a saucepan and very gently fry the shallots, or onion and garlic, with the mushrooms until soft, but **not browned**.
2. Add the flour and stir well to make a roux. Continue to cook, stirring, for 1 to 2 minutes.
3. Remove the pan from the heat and add the fish stock slowly, with a ladle, a dribble at a time, stirring vigorously. Return the pan to the heat and gradually add the wine, and then more stock, stirring all the time until you have the consistency of single cream. Continue to cook for 5 or 6 minutes. Set on one side to cool.

LIGHT THE GRILL

If you are piping potato around your dish, do this now and put it under the grill to warm through, then finish the sauce.

4. Separate the egg yolks into a bowl.
5. Whisking briskly, dribble about three ladles of sauce into the yolks.
6. Return this mixture to the saucepan, whisking well to blend into the sauce.
7. Warm through thoroughly over a medium heat, **without boiling**.

TO POACH THE FISH

1. Bring the court-bouillon to the boil in a pan large enough to hold and cover the fish.
2. Reduce the heat to simmer and put in the fish fillets. Cook for 3 to 4 minutes.
3. Remove the fish with a slice, so it drains, and place on a hot serving dish or inside your potato ring.
4. Dress the fish with the sauce and place under the grill to lightly brown.

TO SERVE, garnish with freshly chopped parsley.

MACKEREL POACHED IN WHITE WINE À LA PROVENÇALE

A nice easy dish, this brings back memories of a delightful little seaside village near St. Tropez where I first enjoyed dorade, a local Mediterranean fish. Cooked in the regional style, it was delicious! Here I have adapted that recipe for mackerel. It is also suitable for sea bass or mullet, but not herring.

Delicious hot, serve with mashed potato and a green vegetable (broccoli, peas or beans). It is also excellent served cold, with salad, as a main course, as a starter on a bed of salad leaves or part of an hors d'oeuvre.

Fresh mackerel should be firm and bright. Choose medium sized fish, one per person. I have used six fish in this recipe, anticipating a meal for four, with enough left over for a starter or part of an hors d'oeuvre later. For the most economical result I suggest you cook the number of fish required to cover the base of a chosen dish for, if your dish is not covered, you will be wasting wine! You will find a Chasseur rectangular dish is ideal for this recipe. (See illustration p.81)

YOU CAN REHEAT THIS DISH SATISFACTORILY IN A MICROWAVE.

TO SERVE 6 YOU WILL NEED:

6 Fresh Mackerel
1 Lemon
4 Tomatoes
1 Onion
Herbes de Provence
Approx. ¹/₂ Bottle of Dry White Wine
2 Tablespoons Olive Oil
Salt & Freshly Milled Black Pepper

PREPARATION
Trim and wash the fish well.

METHOD
Preheat the oven to 180°C/Gas Mark 4
1. Sprinkle the inside of each fish with the herbs.
2. Place the fish head to tail to cover the base of an ovenproof dish.
3. Slice the lemon, tomato and onion and spread them between the fish. Season with a liberal amount of salt and freshly milled black pepper.
4. Pour over enough white wine to cover and add the oil.
5. Cover with foil and cook in preheated oven for 45 minutes.

SECRET OF SUCCESS: be careful with your timing and do not overcook.

—ooOoo—

SPRATS POACHED IN WHITE WINE

This is an inexpensive light meal or starter (reduce the quantities for a starter). Serve simply with fresh bread and butter. There are so many different breads available now that you can make your own choice. Sadly, sprats are only available from November to March.

TO SERVE 4 YOU WILL NEED:

1k /2lb Fresh Sprats
Dry White Wine
¹/₂ Teaspoon Dried Tarragon
Salt & Freshly Milled Black Pepper

PREPARATION & METHOD
1. Cut off the heads.
2. Slit the underbelly and remove the guts (there is very little to remove) and wash under a running cold tap.
3. Arrange the sprats **in one layer** in a frying pan, or a sauté pan.
4. Season with salt and freshly milled black pepper, sprinkle with tarragon and cover with dry white wine.
5. Cover the pan with a lid and bring gently to the boil. Simmer for 3 minutes.

SERVE hot with crisp bread and butter or cold with salad.

—ooOoo—

SOUSED HERRINGS

This recipe comes from my mother. It is a very old fashioned, simple dish, sometimes confused with rollmop herrings or pickled herring. Soused herrings are not at all the same, they are not filleted or rolled, but poached whole in the oven. They are much sweeter than rollmops.

Served cold, soused herrings make an excellent starter, part of an hors d'oeuvre, or a main course with salad. THEY WILL KEEP WELL IN THE FRIDGE, IN THEIR LIQUID.

TO SERVE 4 YOU WILL NEED:
4 to 6 Herrings
1 Onion
¹/₂ Lemon
1 or 2 Bay Leaves
Malt Vinegar
Water
Whole Pickling Spice
Mild Olive Oil
Salt & Freshly Milled Black Pepper

PREPARATION & METHOD
Preheat your oven to 180°C/Gas Mark 4
1. Trim and wash the fish well.
2. Choose an ovenproof dish about 1¹/₂" deep and large enough to fit a single layer of 4 or 6 fish. I recommend a Chasseur cast-iron, or porcelain, rectangular dish.
3. Lay the fish in the dish and sprinkle liberally with salt and pepper, scatter on the pickling spice.

Break the bay leaves into pieces and add these to the dish.
4. Cut the lemon into pieces and dot among the fish.
5. Peel and slice the onion and add to the dish.
6. Measure enough liquid, ¹/₃ Vinegar and ²/₃ water, to cover the fish.
7. Sprinkle oil over the surface.
8. Place in the preheated oven and cook for 1 hour.

TO SERVE: when cold, remove the herrings from their liquid and serve with salad and fresh bread and butter.

—ooOoo—

FISHERMAN'S PIE

This recipe is something different! A veritable 'fisherman's basket' in a light and delicate sauce, topped with lightly browned slices of potato. Serve with a green vegetable such as peas, runner, broad or French (Kenya) beans.

The quantities of the various ingredients are not crucial. Aim for a mixture of flavours and textures. Mussels, when available, make the pie even better. There need only be a few, but the flavour really enhances the sauce.

When buying the fish, ask for some bones (**not plaice**) and **white** skin to make a fish stock.

IN ADVANCE
❏ Make 600ml /1 pint of Court-Bouillon (see p.90).
❏ Cover the fish bones and skin with water in a saucepan and boil for 30 minutes to make 300ml /

$^1/_2$ pint of stock, or use $^1/_4$ chicken cube dissolved in 300ml /$^1/_2$ pint water.

TO SERVE 4 YOU WILL NEED:

600ml /1 pint Court-Bouillon (p.90)
500gr /1lb Fresh Fish:
(take 250gr /8oz of any two of the following):
Haddock/Cod/Hake/Plaice/Lemon Sole
220gr /7oz Fresh Salmon
125gr /4oz Peeled Prawns
125gr /4oz **Unbreaded** *Scampi or Scallops*
225gr /8oz Fresh Mussels
750gr /1$^1/_2$ lb Potatoes
For The Sauce :
60gr /2oz Unsalted Butter
30gr /1oz Plain Flour
60gr /2oz Gruyere Cheese
1 Small Onion
$^1/_2$ Clove of Garlic
1 Teaspoon Dried Thyme
300ml /$^1/_2$ pint Fish Stock
150ml /$^1/_4$ pint Dry White Wine

PREPARATION

❑ Have 600ml/1 pint of court-bouillon and 300ml / $^1/_2$ pint of fish stock ready.

❑ Peel and boil the potatoes, **leaving them a little firm**, and set aside.

❑ Thaw the scampi and the prawns: remove from their bags and put in a bowl of **tepid** (not hot) water for about 15 minutes.

❑ Wash, scrape and trim the mussels, **discarding any not tightly closed**. (See mussels p.101).

❑ Grate the cheese.

METHOD

Preheat your oven to 180°C/Gas Mark 4.

1. Place the mussels in a shallow saucepan with a little water and bring to the boil with a lid on. Cook until they open and set aside **in their liquid.**

2. In a shallow pan, bring enough court-bouillon to cover the fish, to the boil. Put in the fish and poach it lightly, **being careful only to simmer**, for 3 minutes.

3. Take the fish out with a slice or perforated spoon and remove the skin and any bones.

4. Break the white fish and salmon into small pieces and lay, mixed, in the dish.

5. Shell the mussels, **discarding any that remain closed after cooking** and scatter, with the prawns and scampi, around the dish. Keep the mussel cooking liquid.

NOW MAKE THE SAUCE

1. Peel and finely chop the onion (see p.50).

2. Peel, chop and crush the garlic.

3. Melt half the butter in a thick based saucepan, add the onion, garlic and thyme and fry gently until tender, **without browning.**

4. Add the flour, stir to blend and cook over a medium heat, stirring for 1 minute.

5. Remove the pan from the heat and start by dribbling in the fish stock, stirring all the time. Add a ladle of mussel juice and the wine. Return

the pan to the heat, still stirring all the time, and adding more fish stock if necessary, until you have a sauce slightly thinner than single cream. Continue to cook for 2 to 3 minutes.

6. Add the grated cheese and blend in until melted. Season to taste with salt and freshly ground black pepper.

TO ASSEMBLE THE PIE

1. Pour enough sauce over the fish to thoroughly moisten it. Keep any surplus to add to the pie when serving.
2. Slice the potatoes and overlap them to cover the top.
3. Melt the remaining butter and brush the potato topping.
4. Cook in the preheated oven for 45 minutes.

—ooOoo—

SHELLFISH

Very few cookery books actually tell you how to prepare and cook shellfish. It is well worth buying live shellfish and enjoying its unmatched freshness.

Langoustines and prawns are absolutely wonderful when cooked fresh and eaten before they are quite cold. It is so quick and simple that there is really no reason to buy them ready-cooked.

Cooking crab or lobster is not for the faint-hearted but, in my opinion, we have allowed ourselves to become too isolated from nature and over-sensitive. If you enjoy eating shellfish in a restaurant, there is no reason to feel you cannot prepare it yourself at home! The humane way is to place the crab or lobster in cold water and bring it to the boil. In this way they are put to sleep.

When cooking shellfish the secret of success is to avoid overcooking and to use plenty of salt.

It is nice to set the table with finger bowls and large table napkins, when you will be using fingers. A small slice of lemon in the finger bowl is a nice touch. And also an extra bowl for the discarded shells.

LOBSTER

A lobster weighing up to 500gr / 1lb will serve one person, one about 750gr / 1¹/₂lb, or slightly more, will serve two.

TO COOK THE LOBSTER

1. Take a large pot of water, with about twice as much salt as for potatoes.
2. Drop the lobster in cold and cover (you may need weights or string to keep the lid down). Bring to the boil and then **simmer** for 15 to 20 minutes, depending on size.

TO TEST lift the lobster out, then using a cloth, straighten the tail. If it feels stiff to pull, give it another 5 minutes.

3. Leave in the cooling water for about 5 minutes, then lift out.
4. While still hot, brush the shell with a little oil, which will give it a bright finish. Allow to cool.

TO PREPARE THE LOBSTER FOR SERVING

1. Lay it on a board, belly uppermost and, using a large, sharp knife, slice it in half lengthways. You may have to give the knife a tap with a mallet or hammer to cut through the back shell.
2. Running through the centre of the tail flesh you will see a dark grey pipe. Remove this as, although harmless, it has an unpleasant sharp flavour.
3. The flesh of a lobster is in the tail and claws, so crack open the large claws in several places with nutcrackers or lobster crackers. This will facilitate the removal of the meat when eating.

Apart from the claws, there is only a very small amount of body meat. Before eating, **remove the fern-like 'fingers'** wrapped inside the body shell, as these are inedible.

SERVE the lobster on individual plates, with a bowl of fresh home-made mayonnaise (p.22) and plenty of fresh crusty bread and a bottle of chilled white wine. If you have lobster picks, getting into the cracks and crevices will be made easier!

SECRET OF SUCCESS: do not overcook. For perfection, serve when not quite cold. Lobster tastes so much better when it has not been refrigerated.

—ooOoo—

CRAB

A 1k to 1¹/₂k/2lb to 3lb male, or cock, crab is considered best. Cock crabs have larger claws than females. A crab of this size will serve two.

The young son of a friend, on a visit ashore during a sailing trip to Dieppe, ordered 'Crabe Parisien'. When the whole crab was set in front of him, he looked flummoxed! Luckily he was sitting next to my late wife who, being Bretonne, was able to show him how to tackle the beast!

At home, we like to eat crab somewhere between 'Parisien' and the fully prepared English style. We make a virtue of the time it takes to pick the feelers and claws ourselves and do not mind at all using our fingers! It is a meal to be sat over and savoured, with plenty of fresh French bread and a nicely chilled bottle of muscadet!

TO COOK
1. Take a large pot of water, with about twice as much salt as for potatoes.
2. Drop the crab in cold and cover with a lid, either weighted or tied down. Bring to the boil and then **simmer** for 15 minutes.
3. Leave in the cooling water for about 5 minutes, then lift out, drain and allow to cool.

TO PREPARE THE CRAB FOR THE TABLE
1. Take off all the claws, crack them open with nut crackers or lobster crackers, but leave the meat inside to be picked out at the table.
2. Holding the body shell in one hand and using the thumb of the other hand, prise open the body at the head and remove the ball shaped interior. **Pull off the grey, fern-like "dead men's fingers" which are clustered round the body, as these are inedible**.
3. Scrape the brown meat out of the shell and mash it. If it is too moist, add a few brown breadcrumbs.
4. Cut the body into four chunks, revealing a honeycomb structure containing white meat.

TO SERVE: set the brown meat in the centre of a large serving dish, with the quartered body around it. Surround this with the claws and feelers. Garnish the dish with slices of lemon and lettuce or parsley.

Serve with a delicate home-made mayonnaise (p22). Take your time and don't forget the muscadet!

SECRET OF SUCCESS: is as for all shellfish, use enough salt and do not overcook!

—ooOoo—
DUBLIN BAY PRAWNS (LANGOUSTINE) OR PRAWNS

Langoustine are not often available, but you will find them more easily on the continent so, if you are self-catering, treat yourself. If you can't find langoustine, substitute fresh prawns in the shell, they are very nearly as good and not so expensive.

Both langoustine and prawns are very simple to cook, just place them in a pot of fast boiling, **well salted**, water and boil for 2 to 4 minutes depending on size. Drain and allow to cool and eat them before they are quite cold.

What could be easier? Only minutes to prepare, it is the perfect meal when you come back from the beach or pool, to eat al fresco. Simply serve with fresh home-made mayonnaise (p22) and crusty bread and butter, and a good bottle of chilled white or rosé wine.

The flesh is in the tail, so break off the head, open and discard the tail shell, then dunk the meat in the mayonnaise. The French also suck the heads, which are delicious!

SECRET OF SUCCESS: don't overcook and eat while still tepid.

MUSSELS

I was fascinated to see mussel farming in Brittany. In a small bay at low water I counted eight blocks of posts, each about 100 x 100, clustered with mussels. They were being harvested with four tractors and trailers, making their way up and down between the posts, in the early morning sea mist.

In common with all fish and shellfish, mussels **must be fresh!** When fresh, the shells are closed. If the shell is open but closes when tapped, it is still alive. If it remains open, it is dead and **must be discarded**. If a number of shells are slightly open, it is a sign that they are stale, so do not buy. **When cooked the mussels will open — discard any that do not.**

MOULES À LA MARINIÈRE

This is a traditional French recipe from Brittany and can be served as a main course or starter. Here I give quantities for a main course. 1½k/3lb of mussels would provide a starter for 4.

I find the ideal pan for cooking mussels is a large Chasseur shallow casserole, but any large, shallow pan is suitable. (See illustration p.77) **The larger the base of your pan, the easier it will be.** If the pan is small, you will need to turn the mussels during cooking with a perforated spoon. If you do not have a pan large enough, cook the mussels in two batches.

TO SERVE 4 YOU WILL NEED:
2k/4½lb Mussels
½ Medium Onion or 3 Shallots
½ Clove of Garlic

300ml /½ pint Dry White Wine
300ml /½ pint Water
30gr /1oz Unsalted Butter
2 Teaspoons Chopped Fresh Parsley
75ml /3fl.oz Cream (optional)

PREPARATION
- Put the mussels into a sinkful of cold water. Thoroughly clean and inspect each mussel, making sure they are all closed. **Discard any that are open or feel heavy.** Pull off the 'beards'. **Lift the mussels, rather that tip them, from the sink or bowl in which you have washed them, so as to leave behind any grit.**
- Finely chop the onion or shallot (see method p.50).
- Crush the garlic.

METHOD
1. Melt the butter in a large, shallow pan and fry the onion and garlic until soft. **But do not brown.**
2. Turn the heat to high, add the water and wine, bring to the boil and add the mussels. Cover with a lid and cook on a high heat, shaking the pan from time to time. It may be necessary to turn the mussels with a spoon. The cooking process will take about 3 to 4 minutes. Mussels are cooked when they open. **Discard any that do not do so.**
3. Lift the mussels with a perforated spoon into individual dishes.
4. Add the cream to the cooking liquid (optional) and stir to blend. Cook fast for about 1 minute.
5. Pour the liquid over the mussels and sprinkle with

chopped parsley.
SERVE IMMEDIATELY with plenty of fresh crusty bread! (and a dry, crisp white wine!)

To eat, remove the mussel with a fork or the shell of another mussel. And a soup-spoon for the juice!

—ooOoo—

SCAMPI À LA PROVENÇALE

Scampi is the tail of a Dublin Bay prawn or langoustine. When sold frozen they are most usually available breaded. However you should be able to track down a source of unbreaded scampi. They are sold in 500gr / 1lb packs and in three sizes, standard, gourmet and jumbo. I usually buy the gourmet size.

Scampi provençale is served with plain boiled rice, so ALLOW YOURSELF ENOUGH TIME TO START COOKING THIS IN ADVANCE (see p.53). Make the sauce in advance, or take it from the deepfreeze. You can also serve a green vegetable like runner or French (Kenya) beans or broccoli.

For a starter, no rice is necessary and 500gr / 1lb of scampi will serve 4.

TO SERVE 4 YOU WILL NEED:
*750gr /1^1/$_2$ lb Frozen **unbreaded** Scampi*
300ml/^{1}/$_2$ pint Provençale Sauce (see p.19)
Mild Olive Oil
1 glass White Wine
12 Black Olives (optional)
Fresh Parsley

PREPARATION
Take the scampi out of the packet and put them into **tepid** (not hot) water to quickly thaw. This takes about 15 minutes. **This method will retain the juices which drain away if thawed slowly, but use immediately.** When thawed, drain and **remove any thin black pipes**, as these have an unpleasant taste.

METHOD
1. Heat a little olive oil in a frying pan and quickly fry the scampi for 2 minutes.
2. Add the sauce and 1 glass of white wine and simmer for 3 minutes.

TO SERVE, decorate with chopped parsley and halved black olives.

SCAMPI MEUNIÈRE

This simple dish can be served as a starter or a main course. I use 'gourmet' size frozen **unbreaded** scampi. A 500gr /1lb pack will make 4 starter portions.

For a main course, serve with new or sauté potatoes and peas, beans or spinach.

TO SERVE 4 YOU WILL NEED:
*750gr /1¹/₂ lb Frozen **unbreaded** Scampi*
Plain Flour
125gr /4oz Unsalted Butter
Mild Olive or Groundnut Oil
1 Lemon
Salt & Freshly Milled Black Pepper
Freshly Chopped Parsley

PREPARATION
❑ Remove the scampi from its packet and put into **tepid** (not hot) water for 15 minutes. **This method will retain the juices which drain away if thawed slowly, but use immediately**.
❑ Cut 4 slices of lemon for decoration. Squeeze the juice from the other half of the lemon and set on one side.

METHOD
1. Put 90gr /3oz of butter ready in a small saucepan.
2. Heat 30gr /1oz of butter and a little oil in a frying pan.
3. Dust the scampi with flour and, when the butter and oil is sizzling hot, sauté them, turning them as they become golden brown, about 3 or 4 minutes. Season lightly with salt and freshly milled black pepper while they are cooking.
4. Place onto a warm serving dish, or divide onto individual plates.
5. Bring the butter in the saucepan to the boil, add the lemon juice and, as it froths, spoon this sauce over the scampi.

TO SERVE, decorate with a sprinkling of parsley and a lemon slice for each portion.

—ooOoo—

MEAT, POULTRY & GAME

preparation and methods explained, with recipes

ROASTING — POT ROASTING — BOILING — GRILLING
FRYING — SAUCE DISHES — CASSEROLING

ROASTING

The most important aspect of roasting is to prepare the joint correctly, to avoid shrinking during cooking, which causes toughness, and to 'seal' the joint to retain the juices. To seal the joint you need a **very hot oven**. It is often believed that a small joint will not roast satisfactorily, but this is not true, small joints can be **seared in a very hot frying pan** before they are placed in the oven and an excellent result achieved.

It is not possible to give exact timings for roasting, as all ovens vary, but you will get to know your own oven and adjust accordingly.

Use a shallow roasting tin or cast iron dish. If you use one that is too deep the heat cannot circulate around the joint so well. This is especially important for pork, when you want good crackling.

Before starting to roast, **make sure that your oven has reached the required temperature**. This must be 230°C/Gas Mark 8 or equivalent for the first 20 to 25 minutes and then reduced to 200°C/Gas Mark 6. Sealing the joint retains the juices and produces a moist result.

It is also important to 'baste' (with a spoon, scoop up the juices in the pan and pour them over the meat) every 20 to 30 minutes. **The hot fat keeps the joint sealed and moist**.

If you have an automatic timer on your oven it may be a boon for a making a casserole, to be ready on your return from work or an outing, but I do not recommend using it for a roast. The result will bear no comparison to a joint cooked by the age old method described above.

Contrary to the advice mostly given, **do not pierce** your joint, chicken or other poultry to test if it is cooked. This releases juices and produces a dry result. **The way to tell if your meat is cooked, is to press the centre**. If it feels soft and spongy, it will be rare. It will feel firm when well cooked. This needs a little practice, but you will soon find you can tell when the joint is done as you like — rare, pink or well done in the middle.

To see if poultry is cooked, squeeze the thick part of the drumstick between your finger and thumb. When you can feel through to the bone it is cooked. **Use a dry rubber glove to avoid burning your hand**.

Most cooks buy ready prepared joints. If you prefer to do so, ask you butcher for some bones to make stock for gravy. Bone stock gravy is a king to that using flavour or colour additives, which can completely spoil a good roast.

It is worth getting to know your butcher or the butchery department in your supermarket. A good butcher knows his customers and aims to please. You will get help in choosing a suitable joint and will be able to ask for bones, or order something special for a celebration. You can, and should, complain if you are dissatisfied and, of course, tell him when pleased.

Joints cooked on the bone generally have more flavour than those that are boned and rolled, but they are more difficult to carve. Whichever joint I choose, for economy and time-saving I usually buy one larger than I require, so that there is enough left over to have cold or make into another dish.

—ooOoo—

ROAST BEEF

Rolled topside, sirloin or forerib are all good roasting joints. If you buy a prepared joint, ask your butcher for some bones to make a stock for gravy. To make a quick stock see p.15. THIS SHOULD BE MADE IN ADVANCE.

If you want to cook on the bone, the best joint to choose is a forerib. It is my favourite for flavour. **Ask the butcher to cut through the chine bone**, so that this can be removed after cooking to make carving easier. If you are prepared to do a little butchery yourself, a forerib is quite easy to bone :

TO BONE A FORERIB:
1. Follow the bone structure with a sharp knife, cutting the meat from the bone.
2. Trim off any excess fat and gristle : lay the meat on a board, skin uppermost. Under the skin, above the 'eye' of the meat, is a layer of gristle. Using a sharp knife, raise the skin and fat, revealing the gristle. Remove as much as possible. **If you do not remove this gristle, the joint will shrink and toughen.**
3. Score the skin in a criss-cross pattern with a sharp knife.
4. Turn the joint on its side and push into a round. Using thin string, tie it into shape at intervals of about 2cm (1").

TO SERVE 4 YOU WILL NEED:
1k to 1¹/₂k /2lb to 3lb Rolled Forerib, Sirloin or Topside
OR 1¹/₂k to 2k /3lb to 4lb Forerib on the bone
60gr /2oz Beef Dripping or Unsalted Butter and Oil
Salt & Freshly Milled Black Pepper
For the gravy
30gr /1oz Plain Flour
450ml /³/₄ pint Bone Stock or made with ¹/₄ Chicken Cube

METHOD
Preheat the oven to 230°C/Gas Mark 8.
1. Make sure your oven has reached temperature. To get a good result it must be **very hot** when you start.
2. Put the dripping or butter and oil in the roasting pan and place it in the preheated oven for 5 to 10 minutes.
3. Remove the pan and roll the joint in the melted fat. Season with salt and black pepper. Put back in the **top half** of the oven for 15 to 20 minutes.
4. Baste the joint, reduce the oven setting to 200°C/ Gas Mark 6. Continue cooking, and baste every 20 minutes.

Allow 15 minutes per 500gr /1lb as a rough guide and an extra 10 minutes per lb for a well done joint.

JUST PRESS TO TEST WHETHER THE JOINT IS COOKED **do not pierce** it.
Without piercing lift the joint out and cover with foil. The joint can 'rest' while you make the gravy, which makes it easier to carve, but I do not advocate leaving it too long.

TO MAKE THE GRAVY

1. Pour most of the roasting fat into a container for dripping, retaining the juices and about a tablespoon of fat.
2. Add the flour to the pan and, with a wooden spoon over a medium heat, stir to form a roux and cook for 1 to 2 minutes. Gradually add the stock, stirring vigorously, until you have the desired consistency. Strain into a gravy boat.

SERVE with roast potatoes, see p.52 Yorkshire Pudding (below), and a root or green vegetable. Particularly good are carrots, parsnips and cabbage.

SECRET OF SUCCESS is a really hot oven to seal the joint and regular basting.

—ooOoo—

YORKSHIRE PUDDING

A real traditional 'batter pudding', light and moist, is made in a roasting or baking dish. However, if you prefer the very airy, puffed up variety, use a sheet of individual muffin moulds.

Sifting the flour is very important, as this will produce a light pudding.

Allow enough time for the batter to "rest" for about an hour. This gives a lighter texture.

Use the dripping from around your joint to coat the roasting dish or moulds.

TO SERVE 4 YOU WILL NEED:

125gr /4oz Plain Flour
1 Large Egg
300ml /¹/₂ pint Skimmed Milk
Pinch of Salt
Beef Dripping

METHOD

1. Sift the flour and salt into a mixing bowl and make a dip in the centre.
2. Break the egg into the flour and, using a **wooden spoon**, stir to gradually incorporate the flour.
3. Slowly add the milk, a little at a time, still stirring. If you are careful you should have a mix with the consistency of single cream and no lumps!
4. Set on one side to 'rest' and then whisk and strain through a sieve.
5. Generously grease your dish or moulds with some of the dripping from around the joint and put into the oven until smoking or blue hot.
6. Ladle the pudding mix into the dish or moulds and replace in the oven, on the top shelf above the joint. Cook for about 35 minutes for large pudding and 20 minutes for individual puddings.

SERVE IMMEDIATELY, standing around will cause the pudding to sink.

Cooking Lamb's Liver
Recipe p.136

ROAST FILLET OF BEEF

If you are feeling extravagant or for a special dinner, order a sirloin fillet from your butcher and prepare it French style.

Allow 185 to 250gr (6 to 8oz) per person.

PREPARATION AND METHOD

Preheat the oven to 230°C/Gas Mark 8.

1. Remove the stringy strip of meat from the side of the fillet and cut off the thin end. (Keep this to add to a casserole or mince).
2. Trim off any skin or gristle and put this in a pan with about 600ml (1 pint) of water and $1/4$ chicken stock cube to make a stock.
3. Tie around the joint to form a log of meat, at intervals of about 2cm (1"), with thin string. This will give you a useful guide for portioning.
4. In a frying pan on a high heat, brown the joint and then cook as for roast beef (p.107).
5. When cooked (**and this joint should be served rare** — see illustration p.113), combine the beef juices with the stock and a little red wine. Take a heaped teaspoon of potato flour, mixed with $1/2$ cup of cold water, and add to the stock gradually until you have good gravy consistency.
6. Carve into fairly thick slices to serve.

—ooOoo—

ROAST LAMB WITH GARLIC AND ROSEMARY

Leg or shoulder of lamb are the most popular joints. You can buy half a large one. Leg is a lean joint and shoulder more fatty. For a smaller joint, loin is excellent. Ask your butcher to chine it and, if he will, to skin it. However, it is not difficult to skin yourself: Using a sharp knife, slice through the skin, taking a line lengthways down the centre of the loin. Use a cloth to give grip and pull off each half towards the thicker chump end.

It is not possible to give exact times, as ovens vary enormously. With practice you will be able to judge by feel when the joint is done as you like it, either pink or well done.

USE THE FOLLOWING AS A GUIDE :

For a loin of lamb, allow 2 or 3 bones per person depending on size. It will only require 35 minutes to cook for a pink result, or up to 1 hour for a well done joint.

A leg weighing $1^3/4$k to 2k /$3^1/2$ to 4lb will serve 6 to 8 people.

A $1^1/2$k /3lb shoulder will give about 5 portions.

Allow approximately 20 minutes per 500gr /1lb cooking time, for leg or shoulder, plus an extra 20 minutes for a well done joint.

Ask your butcher for some bones to make stock for gravy, see p.15.

YOU SHOULD MAKE THIS IN ADVANCE.

The addition of garlic and rosemary gives roast lamb a wonderfully aromatic flavour.

YOU WILL NEED:
Joint of Lamb
Unsalted Butter
Mild Olive Oil
Garlic (optional)
2 Sprigs of Fresh Rosemary (optional)
Red Wine (optional)
Salt & Freshly Milled Black Pepper

PREPARATION & METHOD
Preheat the oven to 230°C/Gas Mark 8.
1. Make sure your oven has reached temperature. To get a good result it must be **very hot** when you start.
2. Place a shallow roasting dish with a good knob of butter and a little oil in the oven.
3. Lightly score the joint with a criss-cross pattern.
4. Skin and cut a clove of garlic, sprinkle it with salt and crush it with the flat of a cook's knife. Smear the garlic salt over the meat, season it with fresh black pepper and sprinkle with rosemary.
5. Paint the joint with the melted butter and oil and put into the oven for 15 minutes.
6. Remove and baste, spooning the butter and oil over the joint. Reduce the oven setting to 190°C/Gas Mark 5 and continue to cook according to weight and times given in the introduction to this recipe, basting every 15 minutes.

TO TEST : when you think the joint is cooked press it, see introduction to roasting.

Remove the joint from the oven without piercing, set on a warm serving dish and keep hot. If it is loin of lamb, remove the chine bone to facilitate carving into chops.

TO MAKE THE GRAVY
Pour off the fat from the roasting dish. Add the wine and a little stock. Using a pastry brush, stir to mix in the browned juices. Cook for 5 minutes and strain.

Serve with mint sauce (see p.21) or redcurrant jelly. Lyonnaise Potatoes and Carrots Vichy (see pages55 & 50) are particularly good with roast lamb.

SECRET OF SUCCESS is a really hot oven to 'seal' the joint for the first 15 minutes of roasting, and regular basting.

ROAST LOIN OF PORK WITH APPLE SAUCE & SAGE & ONION STUFFING

In recent years pork has improved in quality, it has become paler in colour, more tender and better flavoured. Has this something to do with pigs being reared in a more pleasant, outdoor environment? I hope so.

To produce crisp crackling the skin must be deeply scored THROUGH THE SKIN AND FAT. This allows the steam to escape and the heat to penetrate. Butchers rarely score deeply enough to

Guinea-Fowl with Ham Stuffing and Madeira *Recipe p.123*

Roast Fillet of Beef
Recipe p.110

produce crisp crackling, therefore either ask to have your joint scored more deeply or do this yourself with a small, sharp, pointed knife.

Use a shallow roasting dish a deep pan will not produce such good crackling.

My favourite joint of pork is the loin, so my recipe is for this. **Ask for the fore end and ask the butcher to chine the joint.** This will detach the rib bones from the chine or back bone and make preparing the joint easier. If you are feeding a large family, however, a leg, or half a leg, may be better. In this case, score the joint well and start it in a preheated oven at 230°C/ Gas Mark 8 for about 25 minutes and then reduce the heat to 200°C/Gas Mark 6 for a further 45 minutes per 500gr (1lb). Pork should be well cooked.

Roast potatoes around the joint and serve with a green vegetable, apple sauce and sage and onion stuffing.

TO SERVE 4 TO 6 YOU WILL NEED:

1¹/₂k /3lb Loin of Pork
Mild Olive Oil
Unsalted Butter
30gr /1oz Plain Flour
Salt & Freshly Milled Black Pepper

For the Stuffing:
2 Medium Onions
6 Slices Small White Loaf
1 Tablespoon Dried Sage
50ml /2fl.oz Stock
1 Egg
Unsalted Butter

Mild Olive Oil
Salt & Freshly Milled Black Pepper

Apple Sauce:
2 Large (Bramley) Cooking Apples
2 Teaspoons Caster Sugar
Juice ¹/₂ Lemon
Water

PREPARATION & METHOD

Preheat the oven to 220°C/Gas Mark 7.

1. Using a sharp knife, remove the chine, or back, bone from the ribs and any gristle from the back of the joint.
2. Make sure the skin is **deeply** scored. The cuts, in line with the rib bones, and about 1cm (¹/₂") apart, should run the full length of the rind and pierce the skin and fat.
3. Tie with thin string to keep the shape.
4. Season the joint with salt and freshly milled black pepper and paint it with oil.
5. Heat a knob of unsalted butter and about two tablespoons of oil in a **shallow sided roasting dish**.
6. Set the joint in the dish surrounded by roasting potatoes (see p.52 for preparation) and cook for 1¹/₂ hours. Baste at least twice during cooking.

WHILE THE JOINT IS ROASTING MAKE SOME STOCK AND THE STUFFING :

1. Place the bones and gristle in a saucepan and simmer **without a lid** for half an hour or more, to produce stock to moisten the stuffing and for a

114

better gravy.

2. Skin and finely slice the onions.

3. Remove the crusts and crumb the bread in a food processor or with a grater and set aside in a bowl.

4. Place a frying pan on a medium heat with a knob of butter and a little oil. Put in the sliced onion, sprinkle with sage and fry until tender. Season to taste with salt and freshly milled black pepper.

5. Mix the fried onion with the breadcrumbs, moisten with stock, add the egg and mix thoroughly.

6. Place in a small ovenproof dish, dot with 3 small knobs of butter and bake in the oven for ³/₄ hour.

TO MAKE THE APPLE SAUCE:

❏ Peel, core and cut the apples into quarters.

❏ Place in a saucepan of cold water, cover with a lid and bring to the boil. Keep an eye on it and **as soon as it boils** just turn the apple with a spoon to make sure it has all softened a little.

❏ Strain off the water through a colander or sieve and put the apple back into the saucepan and mash with a potato masher. Add the sugar and lemon juice, mix together and transfer to a serving bowl.

WHEN THE JOINT IS COOKED :

1. Set it on a carving dish with the potatoes and keep hot in a low heat oven. **Do not cover**. If you do, the steam will cause the crackling and the potatoes to lose their crispness.

2. Pour off some excess fat from the roasting pan, retaining about 2 tablespoons and all the juices.

3. Set the pan on a medium heat and add 30gr /1oz of plain flour. With a wooden spoon, blend the flour and juices together. Cook for 2 to 3 minutes.

4. Gradually add the stock from the pork bones, stirring well, until you have a good gravy consistency. Strain and keep hot.

SECRET OF SUCCESS is to have the skin and fat well scored to produce good crackling.

—ooOoo—

ROAST DUCK WITH APPLE STUFFING

This was a great favourite in my restaurants, the crispy, well-cooked result being much appreciated. I find Barbary, Debden and Gressingham ducks particularly good for tenderness and flavour and they tend to be less fatty than some others.

You can either use two small ducks or one large. If small, serve each person a half duckling, if large, cut into quarters, or you may prefer to carve rather than joint a large bird.

Because this is a rich dish, plain boiled or creamed potatoes with a green vegetable or celery will go well.

Grilled Lamb Cutlets with Carrots à la Vichy and Lyonnaise Potatoes.
Recipe p.133

Navarin of Lamb
Recipe p.154

TO SERVE 4 YOU WILL NEED:
2 small or 1 large Duckling
Unsalted Butter
Mild Olive Oil
Plain Flour
<u>For the Stuffing:</u>
3 Thick Slices of White Bread
2 Cooking Apples
1 Medium Onion
1 Teaspoon dried Sage
1 Egg
15gr /¼ oz Unsalted Butter
Mild Olive Oil
Salt & Freshly Milled Black Pepper
Watercress to Garnish

IN ADVANCE: Cut off the wing ends, feet and neck of the duck, cover with water in a saucepan and simmer for ½ to 1 hour to make a stock.

PREPARATION AND METHOD
Preheat the oven to 230°C/Gas Mark 8

1. Skin and slice the onion.
2. Peel and grate the apple.
3. Remove the crusts from the bread and make the breadcrumbs in a food processor or with a grater.
4. Melt the butter with a little oil in a frying pan on a medium heat and sweat the onion. Add the apple and a ladle of stock, sprinkle with sage and continue to cook with the lid on for 2 to 3 minutes.
5. Transfer to a bowl and mix in the breadcrumbs. Add and mix in the egg. Season with salt and freshly milled black pepper.
6. Remove any surplus fat from inside the body of the duck wash out and fill with stuffing.
7. THEN TRUSS THE DUCK; with the parson's nose towards you, lay the string across the ends of the drumsticks and taking a turn around the drumsticks, draw them together. Pass the string down each side of the body and take a turn around the wings. Turn the bird over, draw the string taut and tie.
8. Place in a preheated oven for 30 minutes, then reduce to 190°C/Gas Mark 5, baste and continue roasting for a further hour, basting every 20 minutes (allow an extra 20 minutes for a large bird).
When cooked, joint the ducks.

To halve: remove the wishbone and, using a sharp knife, cut along the centre of the breast, following the solid breast bone down to the wing joint. Sever this joint. You should now be able to pull the leg joint out and remove the half duck from the carcass.
To quarter: cut each half in two, slicing at an angle, so that the leg portion includes some breast.

Keep hot while you make the gravy:
❏ Pour off some excess fat from the roasting pan, retaining about 2 tablespoons and all the juices.
❏ Set the pan on a medium heat and add about 2 tablespoons of plain flour. With a wooden spoon, blend the flour and juices together. Cook for 2 to 3

minutes.
- ❏ Gradually add the stock, stirring well, until you have a good gravy consistency. Strain to serve.

Serve each portion of duck with some stuffing and garnish with watercress

—ooOoo—

ROAST DUCK À L'ORANGE

My recipe gives the traditional half a duck per person, crisply cooked.

As for plain roast duck, I use Barbary, Debden and Gressingham ducks wherever possible.

You will require a base brown sauce (see p.16). If you have giblets with your duck, make a stock from these and the necks (see method for chicken stock p.15) and use it in the base sauce. THIS SHOULD BE DONE IN ADVANCE.

TO SERVE 4 YOU WILL NEED:
2 x 1.5k to 1.75k /3lb to 3¹/₂lb Duckling
300ml /¹/₂ pint Brown Base Sauce
45gr /1¹/₂oz Unsalted Butter
Mild Olive Oil
Potato Flour
2 Oranges
90gr /3oz Caster Sugar
2 Tablespoons Red Wine Vinegar
Water
1 Tablespoon of Grand Marnier, Orange Curacao or Brandy
Dried Sage

Salt & Freshly Milled Black Pepper
Watercress to garnish

PREPARATION

Chop off the neck and outer wings of each duck. Cover with water in a saucepan and simmer for ¹/₂ to 1 hour to make a stock. Flush the inside under a running cold tap and dry thoroughly with kitchen paper towel. Sprinkle sage inside the body.

TO TRUSS :
- ❏ Lay the ducks on a board and firmly push each leg forward. **This will shorten the length of the bird, which will improve cooking and its appearance on the plate.**
- ❏ Turn the parson's nose towards you.
- ❏ Lay the string across the ends of the drumsticks and, taking a turn around the drumsticks, draw them together.
- ❏ Pass the string down each side of the body and wrap it round the wings.
- ❏ Turn the duck over, draw the string taut and tie it.

METHOD

Set the oven to 230°C/Gas Mark 8 and **when it has reached temperature :**
1. Place a roasting dish with the butter and a little oil in the oven for 5 minutes.
2. Roll the ducks in the hot fat, season with salt and black pepper and place in the centre of the oven to roast for 1¹/₂ hours. **Baste every 20 minutes.**

Pot Roasted Chicken
Recipe p.122

WHILE THE DUCKS ARE COOKING (OR IN ADVANCE) MAKE THE SAUCE :

❏ Using a zester, potato peeler or small sharp knife, peel the zest (outside skin) of the oranges, **taking care not to include any pith.** Cut into very thin (julienne) strips and set on one side.
❏ Squeeze the juice from one orange and set on one side.
❏ Peel and discard all the pith carefully from the other orange and put this on one side to be sliced for the garnish.
❏ Caramelise the orange zest: place the zest in a small, thick based saucepan, (cast iron is ideal, as it will be less prone to catch and burn) with the sugar, vinegar and water (75ml /5fl.oz) and bring to the boil, stirring to dissolve the sugar. As the water evaporates, the syrup will start to froth. **Have glass of water handy.**

Stir the contents from time to time, until the syrup becomes golden and then **stir continuously as it turns darker.** When it is the colour of mahogany, remove it from the heat and douse with a glass of water. **Take care as the syrup may spit.**

❏ Return to the heat and bring to the boil, ensuring that the syrup has dissolved. Set on one side.
❏ In another pan, combine the base sauce with the orange juice. Add the caramelised orange zest and syrup and the liqueur and simmer for 15 minutes. Season to taste.

TO FINISH AND SERVE :
3. Remove the ducks from the oven and keep warm.
4. Allow the fat to rise to the surface in the roasting pan, and pour off. Add a little stock to dissolve the remaining juices, stir well together and add to the orange sauce.
5. Reheat the sauce and, if necessary, thicken with potato flour (mix a teaspoon of potato flour with $1/3$ cup of cold water and add gradually to the sauce until the desired consistency is reached).
6. Cut each duck in half: remove the wishbone and, using a sharp knife, cut along the centre of the breast, following the solid breast bone down to the wing joint. Sever this joint. You should now be able to pull the leg joint out and remove the half duck from the carcass.

TO SERVE: lay the halves of duck on a hot serving dish, dress with the orange sauce and decorate the dish with the slices of orange and watercress.

SECRET OF SUCCESS : a really hot oven to achieve a crispy result.

—ooOoo—

121

POT ROASTING

In France the ancient method of roasting with a cast-iron casserole was used before the invention of ovens and this simple and economical way of cooking on top of the stove is still widely used. It does not give a crispy result, but the joint will be moist, succulent and full of flavour. Ordinary roasting often produces a dry result, particularly with poultry. It is my favourite way of roasting chicken, veal, tame rabbit and all game birds. An added bonus is that there is no oven to clean!

The meat is first browned in a cast-iron casserole, over a moderately high heat, to seal in the juices, and then, adding only water to prevent burning, the lid is put on, heat turned down and the meat, game or poultry left to cook slowly on top of the stove. A Chasseur cast-iron casserole is a fine addition to any kitchen. Because of its weight and overall heat diffusion it gives a wonderful result.

—ooOoo—

POT ROASTED CHICKEN GUINEA-FOWL OR PHEASANT

If you have not had chicken prepared in this way before, you are in for treat! A dish for all occasions. So easy and economical and yet so wonderfully succulent and tasty! (See illustration p.120) The potatoes are cooked around the chicken and absorb the juices. The recipe and method is the same for guinea-fowl and pheasant.

TO SERVE 4 YOU WILL NEED:

1 Chicken (approx. 1.75k/3$^{1}/_{2}$lb)
500gr /1lb Potatoes
2 Rashers Bacon
2 Tablespoons Olive Oil
Water
Salt & Freshly Milled Black Pepper
Fresh Watercress to Garnish

PREPARATION

❏ Cut the ends off the chicken wings and legs. Put these into a saucepan and cover with water to produce about 300ml/$^{1}/_{2}$ pint of extra stock. Simmer, **without a lid**, for about 30 minutes.
❏ Peel the potatoes and cut into pieces about the size of a walnut.
❏ De-rind and cut the bacon into small pieces.

TO TRUSS THE CHICKEN :

Place the chicken with the parson's nose towards you. Lay the string across the ends of the drumsticks and, taking a turn around the drumsticks, draw them together. Pass the string down each side of the body and wrap it round the wings. Turn chicken over, draw the string taut and tie it.

122

METHOD
1. Heat the oil in a cast-iron casserole and brown the chicken and potatoes on a medium to high heat. Season with salt and black pepper.
2. Add the bacon.
3. Turn the chicken on its back, add 150ml /5fl.oz of water, cover with the lid and reduce the heat to a minimum to simmer for 1 hour.

Check from time to time that the chicken is sizzling but not burning. Add a little more water if necessary.

TO TEST: use a clean, dry rubber glove and squeeze the drumstick. If you can feel the bone, the chicken is cooked.

4. Remove the string and set the chicken on a warm serving dish, surrounded by the potatoes.
5. Add a cup of stock to the casserole and use a pastry brush to mix the browned juices to form a gravy.

TO SERVE : garnish the chicken with fresh watercress and serve with the gravy.

SECRET OF SUCCESS: having just the right amount of water during cooking. Too little and there will not be sufficient steam to cook the chicken, too much and it will casserole rather than roast.

GUINEA-FOWL WITH HAM STUFFING AND MADEIRA SAUCE

This is a super dinner party dish and can be very economically produced, using the breasts and keeping the legs to make a pie. (The recipe for Guinea-fowl, Pork and Mushroom Pie is on p.165)

Using a cast-iron casserole to pot roast (see introduction to this chapter), the result is succulent and full of flavour.

Although quite a complicated dish, if you follow the instructions carefully you will find no snags.

When entertaining, MAKE THE BASIC SAUCE AND THE STUFFING AND STUFF THE BIRDS IN ADVANCE, leaving only the roasting of the guinea-fowl and finishing of the sauce to do before your guests arrive.

TO SERVE 4 YOU WILL NEED:
2 Guinea-Fowl
2 Tablespoons Mild Olive Oil
100ml /4fl.oz Water
Salt & Freshly Milled Black Pepper
For the Stuffing :
185gr /6oz Gammon Steak
1 Medium Onion
2 Teaspoons Dried Sage
100ml /4fl.oz Water
4 Slices (stale) White Bread
1 Egg
60gr /2oz Unsalted Butter
Freshly Milled Black Pepper

For the Sauce :
300ml /¹/₂ pint Basic Brown Sauce (see p.16)
100ml /4fl.oz Madeira
50ml /2fl.oz Double Cream
Freshly Milled Black Pepper
Watercress to Garnish

PREPARATION AND METHOD

First, using a sharp knife, remove the legs and outer wings from the guinea-fowl and set these aside in the fridge or freezer for the second recipe (see p.165).

THEN MAKE THE STUFFING :

❑ Cut the onion in half, remove the skin and cut into small chunks.
❑ Trim and cube the gammon.
❑ Remove the crusts from the bread and make breadcrumbs, either in a food processor or using a grater. Put aside in a bowl.
❑ Melt the butter in a frying pan, add the onion and gammon pieces. Sprinkle with sage, add the water, cover with a lid and simmer for 5 minutes.
❑ Pass the contents of the frying pan through a food processor or mincer and add to the breadcrumbs. Add the whole egg, liberally season with black pepper and mix well.

TO STUFF THE GUINEA-FOWL :

Take the guinea-fowl, wash the cavity and remove any excess fat. Fill with the stuffing.

Tie with string by passing it under the parson's nose, crossing it over and down the sides of the bird and around the wings, then tie it underneath. This will partially close the end of the carcass and help to keep the stuffing inside.

TO COOK THE GUINEA-FOWL:

1. Heat the oil in a cast-iron casserole and place the guinea-fowl in the pot. Brown each side of the breast for 3 to 4 minutes over a medium to high heat. Season with salt and pepper.
2. Turn the guinea-fowl onto their backs. Add the water and cover with lid. Turn the heat down and simmer for 1 hour. Check from time to time that the pot has not boiled dry, adding more water if necessary.

WHILE THE GUINEA-FOWL ARE COOKING, EITHER MAKE A BASIC BROWN SAUCE (see p.16) OR TAKE SOME FROM THE FREEZER AND PUT IT READY IN A SAUCEPAN.

3. When cooked, remove the guinea-fowl from the casserole and keep hot.

TO COMPLETE THE SAUCE :

❑ With a spoon or gravy separator remove any excess fat from the juices in the casserole. Add the juices and the Madeira to your basic sauce, stir and simmer for 5 minutes. **It is important to 'cook out' the alcohol, otherwise your sauce will have a raw taste.** Check for seasoning.
❑ Bring the sauce back to boiling point and add the cream, stirring in well, and cook for 1 minute.

TO SERVE: arrange the stuffing in four mounds on a heated serving dish. Carefully slice the whole breasts (including the wings) of each guinea-fowl from the carcasses and place on top of the stuffing. Press down gently.

Dress each portion with sauce and tuck a small bunch of watercress under each wing to garnish. See illustration p.112.

NOTE: if you are entertaining, you can keep the guinea-fowl hot, covered with foil. **In this case, add the cream to the sauce and dress and garnish the guinea-fowl just before serving.**

—ooOoo—

BOILING

Boiled dishes produce good, old fashioned, economical family meals and the left over cold meats are useful for sandwich making and salads.

The dishes in this chapter are all very simple, so mostly do not include a 'secret of success'. Attention to detail, particularly seasoning, is **the** secret, as indeed it is for all cooking.

To avoid an over salty dish it is important, when cooking salt cured joints, to soak them in cold water for several hours, if possible overnight. If this is not possible, bring the joint to the boil and change the water. Many joints of bacon and ham are sold shrunk wrapped, labelled 'ready to cook', with no mention of soaking. To omit the soaking would be to spoil the dish.

—ooOoo—

BOILED GAMMON WITH PEASE PUDDING AND PARSLEY SAUCE

This is a good old fashioned English recipe. Particularly suitable on a cold winter's day, and very easy!

It is economical to buy a joint slightly larger than required, so it can be eaten hot and then provide additional cold servings. You can also use what is left over to make Ham Florentine (see p.175) or pasta dishes. As cooked ham keeps well for several days it is a very useful standby.

I like to use a gammon joint, as these are leaner and more tender than shoulder. You can buy bacon joints smoked or unsmoked (green). I think smoked has a superior flavour to green. Both are readily available in supermarkets and some butchers.

At Christmas, or for a special occasion, you may want to cook a whole gammon. This will weigh between 6k and 7k / 12lb to 14lb, take 4 to $4^{1}/_{2}$ hours to cook and provide about 20 servings.

ALLOW TIME, WHEN PLANNING, TO SOAK THE GAMMON OVERNIGHT Also, **allow plenty of time for the cooking, as some hams take longer than others**. This will not pose a problem, as ham will keep hot for at least an hour without deterioration.

I use a Chasseur casserole for this dish or a stainless steel stockpot.

TO SERVE 4 YOU WILL NEED:

2k /4lb Gammon Joint
For the Parsley Sauce:
3 tablespoons Chopped Fresh Parsley
30gr/1oz Unsalted Butter
30gr/1oz Plain Flour
300 ml/¹/₂ pint Milk
Cream (optional)
Salt & Freshly Milled Black Pepper
For the Pease Pudding:
250gr /¹/₂lb Yellow or Green Split Peas
30gr /1oz Unsalted Butter
Freshly Milled Black Pepper
Parsley to Garnish

PREPARATION
❏ Remove the joint from its wrapper and soak in cold water for several hours, or overnight if possible, to draw out the brine in which it has been cured.
❏ At the same time, soak the peas in a bowl of cold water.

METHOD
1. Put the soaked peas in a cloth or muslin, gather it up and tie with string, allowing enough space for them to expand by 50%.
2. Rinse the gammon joint and put it in the casserole with enough cold water to cover. Bring to the boil, add the parcel of peas and **simmer** for 2 to 2¹/₂ hours with the lid on. Check the water level from time to time and see that it is simmering but not boiling too fast. **It is important that the water remains simmering all the time, or the peas will spoil, becoming sloppy.**

TO TEST WHETHER THE GAMMON IS COOKED : remove the joint and, using a cloth or old teatowel, try to peel off the skin. If it comes away easily, it is cooked. Remove all the skin, cover with foil and keep hot. If it requires further cooking, return to the pan, simmer for a further 20 minutes and test again.

3. Leave the bag of peas simmering while you make the parsley sauce.

TO MAKE THE SAUCE
1. Melt the butter in a thick based or cast-iron saucepan and add the chopped parsley. Cook, **without browning**, for 2 minutes.
2. Add the flour, to form a roux. Cook over a moderate heat for 2 minutes. It should look like fatty breadcrumbs.
3. Heat the milk in a saucepan and add gradually to the roux stirring vigorously with a wooden spoon and continue adding milk until you have the consistency of double cream. You can add a little cream, especially if you have used skimmed or semi-skimmed milk. Season with salt and freshly

126

milled black pepper.

4. Remove the sauce from the heat and cover the surface with buttered greaseproof paper (or a butter or margarine wrapper) to keep the sauce hot and prevent a skin forming.

TO MAKE THE PEASE PUDDING
1. Lift the parcel of peas into a colander to drain.
2. Melt the butter in a thick based saucepan.
3. Open the parcel and add the, by now mushy, peas.
4. Stir in the butter, season well with freshly milled black pepper and mix thoroughly.

The consistency should be like that of creamed potatoes. If necessary you can continue cooking over a low heat to dry out until the required texture is reached.

TO SERVE: slice the ham and dribble over a little of the stock to moisten. Garnish with a bunch of parsley. Serve the parsley sauce and pease pudding separately.

SECRET OF SUCCESS: for a good pease pudding it is important that the peas do not become sloppy. Make sure that all the time they are cooking, both with the ham and after this has been removed, the water does not go off the boil.

—ooOoo—

BOILED GAMMON WITH PEACH AND MADEIRA SAUCE

This dish is suitable for a simple dinner party or a treat for the family. I have suggested a larger ham than required, in order to leave enough for a second meal.

You will need some Madeira wine and this is surely a wonderful excuse to keep some in the cupboard! I may be biased, having spent my honeymoon in Madeira, but I think this is a much neglected wine, absolutely wonderful as an aperitif, dessert wine or with cheese as a change from port. Being fortified, it keeps as well as sherry, so is not wasteful. My own choice of Madeira is a Duke of Malmsey.

ALLOW ENOUGH TIME TO SOAK THE HAM OVERNIGHT IF POSSIBLE (see introduction to this section) and have your basic brown sauce (p.16) ready prepared or taken from the freezer in time to thaw. Again I use a Chasseur casserole to boil the gammon.

TO SERVE 4 YOU WILL NEED:
2k /4lb Gammon Joint
1 Tin Peach Halves
For the Sauce :
600ml /1 pint Brown Base Sauce
150ml/5 fl oz of Madeira Wine
Salt & Freshly Milled Black Pepper
Fresh Chopped Parsley to Garnish

PREPARATION AND METHOD
1. Soak the gammon joint, rinse it and then cook as in the preceding recipe for boiled ham.

2. Skin and keep hot.
3. Heat the peach halves in a saucepan in their own juice, **without boiling**.

TO MAKE THE SAUCE
Bring the base sauce to the boil and add the Madeira wine. Simmer for 10 minutes.

TO SERVE: carve the gammon and garnish each portion with a peach half. Pour over about half the Madeira sauce and sprinkle with fresh chopped parsley. Serve the remainder of the sauce separately.

Keep strictly to yourself that this dish is so simple it cannot fail! You are sure to win compliments for the sauce.

OX TONGUE WITH PIQUANT SAUCE

Arriving in Le Havre to find our ferry delayed due to rough weather, we were recommended to eat at a small Café Bar on the outskirts of the town. We drove up and down looking and nearly missed the inconspicuous, rather shabby sign. The bar was crowded but, behind a bead curtain, were plain scrubbed wooden tables and an air of simple tranquillity.

The Patron's wife both cooked and served our meal. The greetings came first, then a carafe of good, robust house wine was placed on the table. There was no menu, simply the plats du jour. With true French priority, we kept the same knife and fork for the whole meal, but enjoyed the luxury of large linen table napkins!

Tomato salad and saucisson was followed by ox tongue in a sauce which inspired this recipe. The whole meal was rounded off by a selection of perfect Normandy cheeses. Have I made your mouth water? Good! The bill was modest too!

Ox tongue, cooked in the French way, is not moulded and pressed. It is quicker and easier to prepare than by the English method, but you will need forward planning to ALLOW TIME FOR SOAKING AND COOKING.

The piquant sauce is very easy. You can make the base sauce (see p.16) in advance or, if you have some in the deep freeze, take it out in time to thaw.
Ask your butcher for a whole ox tongue, or you will find they are available in most supermarkets.

After having the tongue hot with sauce, it will do another meal or two cold. It is excellent on its own or with other cold meats and salad.

TO SERVE 4 YOU WILL NEED:

1 Ox Tongue
2 Teaspoons Whole Pickling Spice in a Sachet (see p.23)
2 Bay Leaves
2 Sprigs Thyme or 2 tsp. dried
2 Sprigs of Parsley
For the Sauce:
600ml /1 pint Brown Base Sauce (see p.16)
10 Small Gherkins
1 Teaspoon Whole Black Peppercorns
100ml /4fl.oz White Wine
1 Tablespoon Red Wine Vinegar
Fresh Chopped Parsley

PREPARATION
Soak the tongue overnight in cold water.

METHOD
1. Remove the tongue from the water and place in a cast-iron casserole or saucepan. Cover with cold water and add the herbs and spice sachet.
2. Bring to the boil and simmer **with the lid on** for 4 hours. Check the water level from time to time and top up from a kettle of boiling water as necessary.

To check whether the tongue is cooked, lift out onto a dish and, using a cloth, try to remove the skin. If it comes away easily it is cooked but, if not, continue to cook for a further $\frac{1}{2}$ hour.

3. When cooked, remove the skin and keep hot covered with foil.

TO MAKE THE SAUCE :
❏ Heat the brown base sauce to boiling point.
❏ At the same time, in a separate pan, boil the white wine, vinegar and peppercorns for 5 minutes and reduce by half. **Do not boil too quickly**, or the liquid will reduce before the peppercorns have had time to infuse. It may be necessary to add a little water to prevent the liquid reducing too quickly.

❏ Strain the reduced liquid through a sieve into the brown sauce and stir to blend.

Just before serving, chop the gherkins and add, with freshly chopped parsley, to your sauce.

TO SERVE: carve the tongue, not too thin, starting at the thick end. Pour some of the sauce over the sliced tongue and sprinkle with freshly chopped parsley. Serve the remainder of the sauce separately.

SECRET OF SUCCESS is in making the liquid for the sauce. Boiling removes the raw taste from the wine and vinegar and the reduction intensifies the flavour.
—ooOoo—

FRICASSÉE OF TURKEY
A fricassée so often means cold chicken or turkey leftovers, warmed up in a bland white sauce with added mushrooms! Try this recipe and appreciate the difference. It is a wonderfully delicate dish of tender turkey pieces poached and then served in a creamy sauce, thickened with egg and a subtle taste of lemon.

You can use either fresh turkey breasts and cut these into 'bite sized' pieces, or ready-diced turkey as available at supermarkets. You can also vary the recipe by using chicken breasts.

I like to serve fricassée on a bed of rice (see p.53) with a fresh green vegetable like broccoli.

TO SERVE 4 YOU WILL NEED:

750gr /1¹/₂lb Diced Turkey Breast
375gr /12oz Button Mushrooms
2 Medium Onions
900ml /1¹/₂ pints Water
¹/₂ Teaspoon Salt
1 Sprig Thyme or ¹/₂ tsp dried
1 Sprig Parsley
1 Bay Leaf
1 Teaspoon Whole Pickling Spice in a Sachet (see p.23)
¹/₂ Chicken Stock Cube
45gr /1¹/₂ oz Unsalted Butter
45gr /1¹/₂oz Plain Flour
2 Egg Yolks
Juice of ¹/₂ Lemon
Salt & Freshly Milled Black Pepper
Fresh Chopped Parsley to Garnish

PREPARATION

❏ Cut the onions in half, remove the skin and cut into small chunks.
❏ Wash the mushrooms.

METHOD

1. In a cast-iron casserole or large saucepan boil the water, with the herbs, spices, salt and ¹/₂ chicken cube. Add the turkey and onion, turn the heat to simmer for 35 minutes with a lid on.
2. Add the mushrooms and continue to simmer for a further 15 minutes.

3. Strain the liquid through a sieve into a bowl or container, retaining the turkey, mushrooms and onions in the casserole, but removing the herb sprigs and spice sachet. Keep hot.
4. Melt the butter in a thick based saucepan over a medium heat. Add the flour and stir in with a wooden spoon. Cook for 2 to 3 minutes.
5. Gradually add the stock, **a little at a time**, stirring briskly to avoid lumps, until you have a fairly thin sauce consistency. Continue cooking for a further 10 minutes.
6. Put two ladles of this sauce into a bowl to cool.
7. Squeeze the juice from half a lemon.
8. Separate the egg yolks into another bowl, add the lemon juice and whisk together.
9. Now, whisking all the time, combine the egg mixture with the **cooled** sauce.
10. Take this mixture and, again whisking vigorously, add it to the hot sauce. (If necessary, reheat your sauce **but do not boil**. Check the seasoning.
11. Pour the sauce over the turkey and mushrooms, stir together and put into a serving dish.

TO SERVE: if you want to keep this dish hot, place the serving dish in a container of water in a warm oven and make sure it does not boil.

SECRET OF SUCCESS is to be speedy in the amalgamation of the egg and lemon mixture with the cool sauce, and again when incorporating this into the hot sauce. The danger is for the egg to curdle.

—ooOoo—

GRILLING

Correct preparation of the meat before grilling is of paramount importance. If sinew, membrane and gristle are not either removed or cut before cooking, the meat with shrink up and toughen.

Most domestic grills, gas or electric, are not man enough to produce a first class result with meats, particularly steaks. To overcome this problem, I recommend using a Chasseur cast-iron grill pan.

There are two methods that can be used :

1. Use the grill pan on top of the stove only and a lid to cover the meat to speed cooking.
2. Use both the grill pan and the grill. Finishing the meat under the grill.

Both methods have similar timing. Exact times will depend on your hob and grill and should be adjusted accordingly.

The most important aspect is to have both your grill and your pan really hot before starting to cook the meat. Speed is the key to success when grilling.

Steaks and other grilled meats are best served with sauté or new potatoes and either a fresh green vegetable or a salad.

I use a good quality mild olive oil or groundnut oil for grilling, but you can, if you prefer, use clarified butter (see p.26). When using oil, make sure it is fresh, as stale oil will spoil the flavour of your grill.

<u>Deglazing</u>: A delicious and easy 'jus' or gravy is made by '**de-glazing**'. This is done by simply adding a little wine to the juices left after grilling steaks or chops and boiling to reduce a little and cook out the alcohol. The 'cooking out' is important, or you get a raw flavour. For a slightly thicker 'jus', simply add a knob of unsalted butter and stir when boiling.

—ooOoo—

GRILLED FILLET STEAK

PREPARATION AND METHOD

If you wish to finish your steak under the grill, turn it on to heat in plenty of time.

1. Trim off all gristle.
2. Paint the grill pan with a little oil and heat until sizzling.
3. Brown the steak on each side for about 1½ minutes to seal in the juices, seasoning with salt and freshly ground black pepper.
4. Continue cooking, with a lid or under a preheated grill (see methods 1 & 2 in the introduction), turning once, until done as required :

Rare :   2 to 4 minutes.
Medium: 5 to 6 minutes
Well Done : 8 to 10 minutes.

For a very well done fillet steak, I 'butterfly' the meat. Simply cut about ¾ the way through the middle of the steak, across the grain. Open it up and press flat before cooking. Done this way, the steak will cook quicker and therefore retain more juice and flavour.

If you like gravy with your steak, you can de-glaze the pan : see introduction to grilling.
TO SERVE, garnish with fresh watercress.

GRILLED ENTRECÔTE OR RUMP STEAK

PREPARATION & METHOD

If you wish to finish your steak under the grill, turn it on to heat.

1. Trim any gristle from the lean side of the steak.
2. There is a line of gristle between the fat and the meat. Cut through the fat and gristle at right angles to the steak, at intervals of about 2.5cm (1"), using a sharp knife onto a chopping board. **This will prevent the gristle contracting and drawing the flesh tight and the result will be more tender**.

Then follow 2, 3, 4 for Grilled Fillet Steak.

You can de-glaze the pan: see page 131.

TO SERVE garnish with fresh watercress.
—ooOoo—

MINUTE STEAK

This is a trimmed entrecôte steak of about 155gr /5oz, flattened to about 0.5cm (¼").

Simply brown it quickly on a **very hot** grill pan, brushed with oil, 1 minute each side. Season with salt and freshly milled black pepper.

You can de-glaze the pan : see page 131.

TO SERVE garnish with watercress.

—ooOoo—

GRILLED LAMB CHOPS OR CUTLETS

As with all grilled meats, it is important to carefully prepare the chops or cutlets by trimming away all excess fat and gristle, to prevent them curling up and toughening.

For dinner party presentation, chop and cut away the piece of backbone, leaving just the rib bone trimmed (see illustration p.116).

Allow three chops per person.

Lamb chops are best lightly grilled, so I only use the grill pan and a lid.

METHOD

1. Paint the grill pan with a little oil and heat until sizzling.
2. Brown the chops on both sides. Season with salt and freshly milled black pepper and continue cooking, covered with a lid, turning once until done as required. Timing will depend on personal taste and the thickness of the chops. I like mine pink so, having browned them, just one minute extra cooking is sufficient.

If you like gravy with your chops, you can de-glaze the pan: see p. 131.

Serve with Carrots Vichy or French Beans and Lyonnaise Potatoes with a sprig of fresh watercress.

—ooOoo—

GRILLED PORK CHOPS

Pork chops, particularly thick ones, take longer to grill. I find using a grill pan and lid to cover the best method. The lid speeds the process and the result is more moist than lengthy grilling.

Preparation is very important to prevent shrinking and toughening.

METHOD & PREPARATION

1. You will find, under the fat surrounding the meat, a layer of gristle. Slice through the fat and gristle at intervals of about 2.5cm (1") at right angles to the chops.
2. Paint the surface of the grill pan with oil and place on a high heat.
3. When sizzling hot, add the prepared chops, season with salt and freshly ground pepper and brown for 3 minutes.
4. Turn and after 2 minutes reduce the heat and cover with a lid. Continue cooking for about 5 to 6 minutes.

It is important that the chops are cooked through and not pink.

You can de-glaze the pan for a nice "jus" — see p.131.

TO SERVE, garnish with a sprig of fresh watercress.

—ooOoo—

133

FILLET STEAK STUFFED WITH STILTON

The combination of tender steak surrounded with bacon and stuffed with melting stilton makes this a substantial, special occasion dish. Ask your butcher for a tournedos, cut from the thinner end of the beef fillet.

This steak should be served medium. Overcooking will cause the cheese stuffing to disappear and the character of the dish will be lost.

YOU CAN USE A LITTLE OLIVE OIL INSTEAD OF CLARIFIED BUTTER IF YOU PREFER, or unsalted butter with a little oil.

TO SERVE 4 YOU WILL NEED:

4 x 250gr /8oz Tournedos Steak
4 Rashers of Streaky Bacon
125gr /4oz Blue Stilton Cheese
45gr /1½oz /Clarified Butter (see p.26)
150ml /6fl. oz Red Wine
Knob of Unsalted Butter
Salt & Freshly Milled Black Pepper
Watercress to Garnish

PREPARATION

❑ Trim any skin or membrane from each steak.
❑ Make a deep incision, from the side, across the grain, into the centre of the steak, to form a pocket for the stuffing.
❑ Divide the Stilton into four and stuff into the pocket in each steak.
❑ Remove the rind from the bacon and flatten each rasher with the flat of a cleaver or heavy knife. Wrap a rasher around each steak. Draw the bacon fairly tight and secure it with a cocktail stick.

METHOD

1. Place a frying pan on a medium to high heat. Add the clarified butter and, when sizzling, add the steaks. Brown each side for 2 to 3 minutes. Season with a little salt and black pepper while cooking.
2. Turn down the heat and cover the pan with a lid. Continue to cook for 5 to 6 minutes, until the cheese is melted and oozing.
3. Remove the cooked steaks to a warm dish and keep hot.
4. Add the wine to the pan, turn up the heat and bring to the boil. Using a pastry brush, mix the wine with the juices. Stir in a knob of unsalted butter to slightly thicken the sauce and then pour over the steaks.

TO SERVE garnish with fresh watercress.

—ooOoo—

FRYING

I am assuming that my readers have all done quite a bit of frying! Eggs and Bacon, Sausages, Steaks, Chops, Liver and Kidney can all be fried. In this section I give some recipes that, besides using the basic method of frying also use flaming and de-glazing.

By burning off the alcohol, flaming gives an enhanced, mellow flavour to a dish.

As with grilling a delicious and easy 'jus' or gravy is made by de-glazing.

To achieve excellence I recommend you use a cast-iron frying pan, which will distribute the heat evenly. Chasseur frying pans and skillets can be used on any stove and at very high temperatures, allowing you to sear and seal meats when required.

—ooOoo—

PEPPERED STEAK (STEAK AU POIVRE)

My first memory of a peppered steak was of a supremely tender steak, dressed with a brandy and butter glaze with green peppercorns. This dish is sometimes varied, using black peppercorns and cream in the sauce, but I still prefer the original, traditional recipe.

It is important to use clarified butter. I use jars of green peppercorns as, once open, these can be kept in the fridge, unlike tins.

TO SERVE 4 YOU WILL NEED:
4 x 250gr /8oz Entrecôte or Fillet Steak
4 Tablespoons Green Peppercorns
45gr /1¹/₂oz Clarified Butter (see p.26)
60gr /2oz Unsalted Butter
80ml /3fl.oz Good Brandy
Salt & Freshly Milled Black Pepper
Watercress to Garnish

PREPARATION
- ❏ Cut the unsalted butter into cubes.
- ❏ Trim any fat or gristle from the steaks.
- ❏ Using a pestle and mortar, or a wooden rolling pin and board, crush the green peppercorns and then press them firmly into both sides of the steak. The steaks should be well coated.

METHOD
1. Heat the clarified butter in a frying pan over a medium to high heat. When sizzling hot, add the steaks and cook for 2 to 3 minutes on each side, seasoning with salt and pepper.
2. Remove the pan from the heat and FLAME WITH BRANDY: (see p.68).
3. When the flames have died down, remove the steaks and keep warm. Return the pan to the heat and gradually add the knobs of butter, stirring to form a glaze.

TO SERVE, spoon the glaze over the steaks and garnish with watercress.

SECRET OF SUCCESS: green peppercorns give a pleasant, mild taste and flaming with brandy develops and mellows the flavour of the glaze.

—ooOoo—

LAMB'S LIVER AND BACON

A lady once paid me the compliment "You are the best liver cooker I have ever known — and I am very old!". She was not, of course, and she was herself a cook of some repute! So here is the secret: **prepare the liver carefully.**

Preferably buy your liver in a piece, not ready sliced, and only buy fresh English lamb's liver, as any other has been frozen, will be pappy and inclined to be too strong in flavour.

TO SERVE 4 YOU WILL NEED:
500gr /1lb Fresh Lamb's Liver
8 Rashers Bacon
2 Medium Onions
Mild Olive Oil or Unsalted Butter and a little Oil
3 Tablespoons Chopped Parsley
150ml /5fl.oz Red Wine
Flour
Salt & Freshly Milled Black Pepper
Watercress to Garnish

PREPARATION
❏ You need to remove the membranous skin and cut away the pipes and sinew from the liver. You can afford to be quite drastic as liver is inexpensive. *To remove the skin*: cut a small flap, insert your thumb and gradually work across the surface, easing the skin off. This can be quite difficult at first but gets easier with practice. If you do buy ready sliced liver, remove the skin by inserting a knife under it and run it round the slices, **blunt side forwards.**
❏ Cut the skinned liver into medium thick slices.
❏ Remove the bacon rind.
❏ Skin and slice the onions.

METHOD
1. Heat a little olive oil or butter and oil in a frying pan and, when bubbling, add the sliced onions. Brown and turn them, then reduce the heat and cover to cook for 4 to 5 minutes.
2. Pop the bacon under the grill, keeping an eye on it and turning when necessary.
3. Remove the onions and keep hot in serving dish.
4. Flour and season the slices of liver with salt and freshly milled black pepper.
5. Add some more butter or oil to the frying pan and turn the heat to high then add the liver. Sprinkle with half the chopped parsley and brown for 2 minutes, turn and sprinkle with remaining parsley and brown for another minute. (See illustration p.109)

Be careful not to overcook the liver or it will toughen, it should remain pink in the centre.

6. Remove and set on a warm serving dish with the onion, adding the grilled bacon.
7. De-glaze the pan: see p.131 and pour over the liver.

SERVE IMMEDIATELY, garnished with watercress.

SECRET OF SUCCESS: take care with the preparation. Use a really hot pan and don't overcook the liver. The addition of fresh parsley makes this recipe 'special' and different.

—ooOoo—

LAMB'S KIDNEYS AND BACON

Lamb's kidneys and bacon, with a crouton to soak up all the wonderful juices, is very simple and quick to prepare and cook.

It is important with all kidney dishes to thoroughly **remove the core and not to overcook**.

Insist on **fresh** English lambs' kidneys. Any others will have been frozen and they will not compare for taste or texture.

TO SERVE 4 YOU WILL NEED:
8 English Lambs Kidneys
8 Rashers of Bacon
4 Slices of Bread (for croutons)
90gr /3oz Unsalted Butter
Mild Olive Oil
150ml /5fl.oz Red Wine
Salt & Freshly Milled Black Pepper

PREPARATION
Heat the grill.
❏ Slice each kidney in half lengthways. Be careful to cut down through the **middle** of the core. Remove the outer membranous skin.
To remove the core: hold the core firmly uppermost. Press your knife down against the flesh of the kidney, pull the core and cut as deeply as possible, to remove the gristly white branches with the core. **Unless you remove the core and the skin of the kidneys, they will shrink up and become tough when cooked.**

❏ Remove the bacon rind.
❏ Cut the crusts off the bread.

METHOD
1. Place the bacon under the grill to cook, turning once. Then keep hot.
2. Heat half the butter and as much oil in a frying pan over a medium heat. Fry the bread until golden brown on both sides and keep hot.
3. Add the remaining butter to the pan on a high heat and, when sizzling hot, add the kidneys, turning and browning for 2 to 3 minutes. Season them whilst cooking with salt and freshly milled black pepper. Remove the kidneys and keep hot.
4. De-glaze the pan: see p131.

TO SERVE Set the kidneys on the croutons surrounded by bacon. Pour over the deglaze sauce. Garnish with watercress and serve immediately.

SAUCE DISHES

For all sauce cooking it is important to use a heavy based saucepan. Copper or Chasseur cast-iron are ideal, as the pans have thick walls as well as thick bases, giving the perfect all-round heat distribution needed. I do not recommend non-stick, as the sauce will be inclined to follow your spoon around the pan, without the friction needed to produce a good sauce.

THE TECHNIQUE OF FLAMING is fully explained on p.68.

To learn how to make a good béchamel sauce, (see p.16) is the key to most sauce making as methods are similar and practice makes perfect. With practice most sauces can be made without weighing the ingredients, the consistency being the guide.

—ooOoo—

CHICKEN BREAST WITH GARLIC, MUSHROOMS AND RED WINE SAUCE

The essential ingredient in this recipe is garlic which, together with red wine, forms a rich flavoured sauce to contrast with the chicken.

Use fresh stock if you have it or substitute water flavoured with a fragment of chicken cube.

This is a really quick and easy recipe.

TO SERVE 4 YOU WILL NEED:
4 Chicken Breasts (boneless)
375gr /12oz Small Button Mushrooms
2 Cloves of Garlic
Plain Flour
Unsalted Butter
Mild Olive Oil
150ml /5fl.oz Red Wine
75ml /3fl.oz Chicken Stock

Salt & Freshly Milled Black Pepper
Freshly Chopped Parsley to Garnish

PREPARATION
❑ Lay each chicken breast on your board, cut side uppermost. Fold the inner section of the breast away from the outside, revealing a very thin membrane and sinew. With a sharp knife make several crossways cuts, severing the cords. Turn the breast over and repeat the process. **This will prevent the chicken pulling up, shrinking and toughening during cooking.**
❑ Skin and cut the garlic, sprinkle it with salt and crush it with the flat of a cook's knife. Smear the garlic salt over the chicken breasts.
❑ Wash the mushrooms.

METHOD
1. Put the flour on a plate and generously flour each breast.

2. Melt the butter and oil in a frying pan on a medium heat until it begins to froth.
3. Add the chicken and season with pepper. Fry for 3-4 minutes and turn.
4. Add the stock, red wine and mushrooms and cover. Reduce the heat and simmer for 12 minutes, checking from time to time and adding more stock or water if necessary. When finished, the sauce should be the consistency of thin gravy.

TO SERVE arrange the chicken breasts on a warm serving dish and dress with the mushrooms and sauce. Sprinkle with fresh chopped parsley.

SECRET OF SUCCESS is cutting the sinew in the chicken breasts, which makes for a really tender result.

—ooOoo—

CHICKEN BREAST WITH MUSHROOMS IN CREAM AND SHERRY SAUCE

This is a very easy dish, but particularly delicious, so will come in for a lot of praise! The sauce is light and delicate and the tenderness of the chicken is frequently remarked upon. **This tenderness is achieved by cutting the sinew and membrane when preparing the chicken. If this is not done the breast pulls up and shrinks and toughens during cooking.**

Ideal for a special meal at the end of a busy day or for entertaining, you can have it on the table in half an hour or less!

The sauce is flamed, and an explanation and full instructions are on p.68.

As the sauce is made in a frying pan, you will find a good, heavy based pan the best, Chasseur once more being ideal.

TO SERVE 4 YOU WILL NEED:
4 Chicken Breasts (boneless)
185gr /6oz Button Mushrooms
Plain Flour
Unsalted Butter
Mild Olive Oil
150ml /5fl.oz Medium Sherry
150ml /5fl.oz Water or Stock
300ml /10fl.oz Double Cream
Salt & Freshly Milled Black Pepper
Freshly Chopped Parsley to Garnish

PREPARATION
❏ Prepare the chicken as p.138 for chicken with garlic, mushrooms and red wine sauce.
❏ Wash and slice the mushrooms.

METHOD
1. Using a plate, **generously** flour each chicken breast.
2. Melt a knob of butter and a little oil in a frying pan on a medium heat until it begins to froth.
3. Add the chicken and season with salt and pepper. Fry for 3-4 minutes and turn.
4. TO FLAME: add the sherry and ignite. Allow the flames to die down a little and douse with the water or stock.

139

5. Add the sliced mushrooms. Place a cover on the pan, turning the heat to low. Simmer for 12 minutes, checking the liquid from time to time and adding a little more stock or water if necessary. **The liquid should be sufficient to prevent the contents sticking to the pan and burning.**
6. Remove the chicken from the pan and arrange on a hot serving dish, leaving the liquid and mushrooms in the pan.
7. Turn your heat back up to medium and reduce the liquid to roughly $1/2$ a cupful. Add the cream and stir until it comes to the boil. Continue cooking until it forms a creamy textured sauce. Check the seasoning.

TO SERVE, pour the sauce over the chicken and sprinkle with freshly chopped parsley.

SECRET OF SUCCESS: flour the chicken generously, to produce a slightly thickened sauce. Be careful to reduce your liquid enough before adding the cream, or it could curdle.

—ooOoo—

ESCALOPE OF PORK NORMANDE

Normandy is often likened to Devon and Dorset and is rich in dairy produce, apples, cider and calvados. Pork Normande uses these products to great effect and is a wonderful special occasion dish.

The apple harvest is in October. Out in the country every smallholding has its orchard and the apples are knocked out of the trees with long sticks and then picked up off the ground into buckets, baskets or wire containers. The youngest and most agile of the picking party climbs the largest trees and shakes them, showering the apples down. In the middle of the day everyone takes a rest under the trees and out comes bread, cheese and paté, to be washed down with some of last year's cider.

The sauce for this dish is flamed, see p.68 for a full explanation and instructions.

TO SERVE 4 YOU WILL NEED:
2 x 375gr /12oz Pork Fillets or Tenderloins
1 Medium Onion
1 Large Eating Apple
Slice of Lemon
Mild Olive Oil
Plain Flour
2 Tablespoons Calvados
225ml /8fl.oz Cider
Approx. 225ml/8fl.oz. Double Cream
Freshly Chopped Parsley
Salt & Freshly Milled Black Pepper

PREPARATION
❑ Peel the apple, keeping the peel, and cut into quarters, removing the core. Cut each quarter, lengthways, into three. Place these into a small saucepan, add a slice of lemon, and cover with water. Bring to the boil, then set aside for the garnish.
❑ Trim the fillets with a sharp knife, removing any skin or sinew.

140

TO MAKE THE ESCALOPES, cut the fillets into half. On a board, stand each half on end and press down with your fingers to start flattening it, cover with clingfilm and flatten with a wooden mallet, rolling pin or the side of a cleaver, until about 5mm (¹/₄") thick.

❏ Score each side of the escalopes with a sharp knife in a criss-cross pattern.

❏ Using a plate, thoroughly coat the pork with flour and season with salt and black pepper.

❏ Skin and finely chop the onion (see method p.50).

METHOD

1. Melt a large knob of butter and a little oil in a frying pan on a medium heat and add the onion.

2. Put the pork into the pan and fry for 2 to 3 minutes on each side, to lightly brown.

3. Flame with Calvados see p.68. When the flames have died down, add the cider and apple peel. Cover and simmer for 10 minutes.

4. Remove the escalopes and place them on a warm dish. Keep hot.

5. Remove the apple peel and boil the remaining liquid to reduce by about half.

6. Add the cream, stirring well, and bring back to the boil. **The cream added should equal twice the volume of the reduced liquid, to produce a sauce the consistency of double cream.** Simmer for 2 minutes.

TO SERVE, decorate each escalope with three pieces of apple and spoon over the sauce and decorate with a sprinkle of fresh parsley.

SECRET OF SUCCESS: make sure you have coated the escalopes in sufficient flour to produce a nicely thickened sauce. Be careful to reduce the liquid sufficiently before adding the cream, or the sauce might curdle.

—ooOoo—

PORK CHOP CHASSEUR

Once I was the butt of my own strange sense of humour! A guest complimented me on the pork chasseur and I responded by saying that it was amazing what one could do with a 'cook-in' sauce! To my chagrin he believed me!

This is another quick and easy dish to prepare and can be varied by using pork fillets, chicken breasts or steak.

ALLOW ENOUGH TIME (45 minutes) TO MAKE THE CHASSEUR SAUCE OR TAKE IT FROM THE FREEZER IN TIME TO THAW.

TO SERVE 4 YOU WILL NEED:
4 x 250gr /8oz Pork Chops
Unsalted Butter
Mild Olive Oil
300ml /¹/₂ pint Chasseur Sauce (p.19)
Salt & Freshly Milled Black Pepper
Freshly Chopped Parsley

PREPARATION

Under the fat surrounding the meat is a layer of gristle. To prevent the meat from curling and tightening during cooking, slice through the fat and gristle at intervals of about 2.5cm (1") at right angles to the chop. This will give a more tender result.

METHOD
1. Melt a knob of butter with a little oil in a frying pan and, when sizzling hot, add the prepared chops. Cook for about 3 minutes and turn. Cook for a further 2 to 3 minutes.
2. Add a little water, season with salt and black pepper, cover and simmer for 10 minutes.
3. Remove the chops and set them on a hot serving dish.
4. Add the chasseur sauce to the meat juices in the pan, stir and bring to the boil.

TO SERVE dress the chops with the sauce and garnish with freshly chopped parsley.

SECRET OF SUCCESS is cutting through the fat and gristle of the chop to stop it shrinking.

—ooOoo—

SAUTÉ OF LAMB'S KIDNEYS TURBIGO

Kidneys Turbigo are served on a bed of rice, so an extra green vegetable will be all you need to complete this very attractive dish. As kidneys do not keep hot satisfactorily, you may need to disappear to the kitchen for 10 minutes to perform your magic. However, YOU CAN DO ALL YOUR PREPARATION IN ADVANCE.

TO SERVE 4 YOU WILL NEED:
4 Chipolata Sausages
12 Kidneys
Unsalted Butter
Mild Olive or Groundnut Oil
100ml /4fl.oz Madeira Wine
300ml /¹/₂pint Double Cream
375gr /12oz Long Grain Rice
Salt & Freshly Milled Black Pepper

PREPARATION
Turn on the oven to warm.
COOK THE RICE IN ADVANCE and drain well (see p.53). Place the cooked rice in a lightly buttered ovenproof serving dish, covered with foil, in a medium oven to warm through.
❑ Grill the chipolatas and set aside to keep warm.
   WHILE THE CHIPOLATAS ARE GRILLING, PREPARE THE KIDNEYS: see p137. Slice each kidney half into three.

METHOD
1. Heat a large knob of butter and a little oil in a frying pan and, when sizzling hot, add the kidneys. Turn and brown them quickly for 1¹/₂ minutes, seasoning with salt and freshly ground black pepper.
2. TO FLAME: remove the pan from the heat, add the Madeira and ignite.
3. When the flames have died down, remove the kidneys and keep hot.
4. Return the pan to the heat and boil until the liquid has reduced by half.

5. Add the cream, stirring well and boil until the sauce thickens to the consistency of double cream.
6. Return the kidneys to the pan, check the seasoning and stir together for 1 minute.

SERVE IMMEDIATELY on a bed of rice, garnished with the chipolatas cut into quarters or eighths.

SECRET OF SUCCESS is removing all core and gristle, so that the kidneys do not shrink and toughen. Do not overcook the kidneys.

—ooOoo—

CASEROLING

In this section I have selected a number of recipes which illustrate the wide variety of textures and flavours that can be achieved. They all use much the same method of preparation and cooking, but with different basic materials.

Casseroles take a bit of time to prepare but, once in the oven, you can relax. They are ideal for carefree entertaining, as they can be made in advance. It is also worthwhile cooking extra portions to set aside in the freezer for a quick meal another day.

I have, in most of these casserole recipes, used **potato flour** as the thickening agent. It produces a lighter, more easily digested, sauce than plain flour. Using potato flour has an extra advantage for people with wheat allergies.

I like to use fresh herbs whenever possible. Dried parsley is my least favourite of substitutes and I try to avoid it but, if I can't, I use it very sparingly. Dried thyme is more acceptable and I make good use of either fresh or dried thyme in my recipes.

THE TECHNIQUE OF FLAMING is explained in full on p.68.

You will find that a Chasseur casserole produces wonderful casseroles. Having no hole in the lid there is less evaporation and more concentrated steam heat.

CASSEROLE OF CHICKEN IN RED WINE (COQ AU VIN)

The classic Coq au Vin is probably one of the best known dishes from France and makes a wonderful dinner party dish which needs no last minute attention.

One evening, at my holiday hotel in Bournemouth, a lady stopped to say how much she had enjoyed the chicken in red wine "My dear" interjected her husband "that was made with loving care". Such a compliment is worth striving for, so here is the recipe!

You will get the best result if you use a whole fresh chicken and joint it yourself, as the bones add flavour and you will have bits with which to make a stock for your sauce. However, if you are short of time, or prefer to do so, you can use chicken breasts and make your stock from $1/2$ chicken stock cube with 300ml/ $1/2$ pint of water.

The method used includes flaming. See full instructions p68.

TO SERVE 4 YOU WILL NEED:

1 Whole Chicken or 4 Chicken Breasts
375gr /12oz Belly of Pork
2 Rashers of Bacon
300ml /$1/2$ pint Chicken Stock
$1/2$ Bottle of Red Wine
2 Tablespoons Brandy
2 Medium Onions
1 Clove of Garlic
185gr /6oz Button Mushrooms
Unsalted Butter
Mild Olive Oil
Potato Flour
Tomato Puree
2 Bay Leaves
Sprig Fresh Parsley
Sprig Fresh Thyme or $1/2$ tsp dried
Salt & Freshly Milled Black Pepper
Fresh Chopped Parsley to Garnish

PREPARATION AND METHOD

Preheat your oven to 150°C/Gas Mark 2.

1. TO CUT UP THE CHICKEN, remove the outer part of the wings. Push the legs away from the body and cut off. Cut the legs in two at the joint and chop off the shank end of the drumsticks with a cleaver, heavy knife or shears. Slice through each side of the carcass to remove the back. Cut through the breast bone and then cut each breast in two. Poultry shears are ideal for this job.

2. You now have eight pieces of chicken (or four chicken breasts, which can each be cut in two. Place these in a bowl, cover with red wine and set on one side to marinate.

3. Put the wing ends, shanks and the back into a saucepan with $1/4$ chicken cube and 600ml/1 pint of water, simmer for $1/2$ hour **with no lid** to provide your stock.

4. Skin the pork and remove any gristle and bone, then cut into bite-sized pieces.

5. Remove the rind and cut the bacon into small pieces.

Coq au Vin
Recipe p.144

6. Peel and cut the onion into small cubes.
7. Peel, chop and crush the garlic.
8. Heat a large knob of butter and a little oil in a frying pan and fry the onion, garlic, pork and bacon until lightly golden, then place in the casserole.
9. Remove and thoroughly drain the pieces of chicken, **keeping the wine**.
10. Add a little more butter, if necessary, to your frying pan and, when sizzling, fry the chicken pieces, turning them until golden brown.
11. NOW FLAME WITH BRANDY: See p.68. Allow the flames to die down.
12. Add the chicken and juices to the casserole, together with the herbs, mushrooms and the red wine. Strain the stock and, using 300ml/$\frac{1}{2}$ pint , stir in 2 teaspoons of tomato puree. Add this to the casserole. Season with salt and freshly milled black pepper. Cover and cook in the preheated oven for 1$\frac{1}{2}$ hours.

TO THICKEN THE SAUCE

❏ Ladle the liquid from the casserole into a saucepan. Place over a moderate heat and bring to the boil.
❏ Put 1 heaped teaspoonful of potato flour in $\frac{1}{2}$ a cup of cold water and stir until well mixed.
❏ Slowly pour, a little at a time, into the boiling liquid, stirring briskly, until the sauce is thickened to the consistency of gravy. Simmer for 2 to 3 minutes. Return to the casserole and blend in. Check the seasoning.

TO SERVE, sprinkle with fresh chopped parsley. See illustration p.145.

SECRET OF SUCCESS: flaming with brandy is the key, as with any wine dish, to the special mellow flavour. Just make with loving care!

—ooOoo—

CASSEROLE OF CHICKEN BREASTS WITH LEEKS

Many cooks feel that, in order to reach great culinary heights, it is necessary to spend long hours in the kitchen making complicated dishes. Not at all! Often the most simple is the most effective. I think you will like the delightful combination of flavours in this very easy dish!

TO SERVE 4 YOU WILL NEED:
4 Chicken Breasts
4 Medium Leeks
1 Medium Onion
Unsalted Butter
Mild Olive Oil
600ml /1 pint Chicken Stock
1 Teaspoon Whole Pickling Spice
Sprig Fresh Thyme or $\frac{1}{2}$ tsp dried
1 Bay leaf
Sprig Fresh Parsley
Potato Flour
Salt & Freshly Milled Black Pepper

PREPARATION

Preheat your oven to 150ºC/Gas mark 2.

❏ Cut each breast into three pieces.
❏ Trim and wash the leeks **holding them upside-down under the running tap**, to wash the grit out! Use as much green as white and cut into chunks.
❏ Peel the onion and cut into small cubes.
❏ Put the pickling spice into a sachet (see p.23) **removing the red pieces of chilli.**

METHOD

1. If you don't have fresh stock, make a stock with 600ml/1 pint of water and ¹/₂ chicken stock cube.
2. Put a large knob of butter and a little oil (or you can use oil only) in your frying pan, using a high heat. When it is bubbling, add the chicken pieces and onion and fry, turning, until they are golden brown. Season them while cooking with salt and freshly milled black pepper.
3. Place the chicken and onion with the leeks in a cast-iron casserole. Add the spice sachet, herbs and stock. Put on the lid and cook in a preheated oven for 1¹/₂ hours.
4. Remove the spice sachet, large herb sprigs and bay leaf.

TO THICKEN THE SAUCE

❏ Ladle the liquid from the casserole into a saucepan. Place over a moderate heat to bring to the boil.
❏ Dissolve 1 heaped teaspoonful of potato flour in ¹/₂ a cup of cold water and mix well.
❏ Slowly pour, a little at a time, into the boiling liquid, stirring briskly, until the sauce is the consistency of gravy. Simmer for 2 to 3 minutes. Stir the sauce into the casserole and it is ready to serve.

SECRET OF SUCCESS: the spices, very rarely used in today's cooking, add an extra special, subtle underlying flavour.

—ooOoo—

CASSEROLE OF RABBIT IN WHITE WINE (CIVET DE LAPIN)

Rabbit today is a much neglected white meat. It has a deliciously subtle flavour and is, in my opinion, infinitely superior to chicken.

Growing up, as I did, during the second world war, when meat was short, roast or stewed rabbit was a treat when we could get it. This recipe, however, is another of 'Auntie's' from Paris and is a family favourite.

I prefer to use wild rabbit, for it is a natural food, not artificially reared or fed and has more flavour. But look out for the odd piece of shot when you are eating!

Your butcher will joint the rabbit for you, but he will chop it, which may cause some bone splinters. So it is really better to do this yourself.

If you are using wild rabbits, ALLOW 2 to 3 HOURS TO SOAK THEM IN COLD, SALTED WATER (this removes a rather strong flavour) AND ¹/₂ to 1 HOUR TO MAKE A STOCK.

Ratatouille
Recipe p.54

Peppered Steak
Recipe p.135

TO SERVE 4 YOU WILL NEED:

1 Tame Rabbit (approx.1.5k/2¹/₂lb) or 2 Wild Rabbits
250gr /8oz Belly of Pork
2 Rashers of Bacon
Unsalted Butter
Mild Olive Oil
2 Medium Onions
185gr /6oz Button Mushrooms
2 Bay Leaves
Sprig Parsley
2 Sprigs Thyme or 1 tsp dried
Approx. 300ml /¹/₂ pint Stock
¹/₂ Bottle Dry White Wine
2 Tablespoons Brandy
1 Clove of Garlic
Potato Flour
Salt & Freshly Milled Black Pepper

PREPARATION AND METHOD
Preheat your oven to 150°C/Gas Mark 2.

1. After soaking, wash the rabbit thoroughly under a running cold tap.
2. Using a large sharp knife, cut off each leg.
3. If you feel along the backbone there are dips and mounds. To avoid the bones, slice through the top of the mounds. First remove the tail end, then cut the back into 4 pieces.
4. Put the head, rib cage and tail end into a saucepan and boil, **without a lid**, for ¹/₂ to 1 hour to make a stock. (If you make stock with the lid on it will be cloudy). **Keep the liver**.
5. Remove skin, bone and gristle from the pork and cut into bite-sized pieces.
6. Remove the rind and cut the bacon into small pieces.
7. Skin and slice the onion into small chunks.
8. Skin and crush the garlic.

TO ASSEMBLE THE CASSEROLE:

1. Place a large frying pan on a medium heat with a little butter and oil and fry the onion and garlic until lightly browned. Transfer to cast-iron casserole.
2. Add a little more butter and oil if necessary and, when sizzling, fry the pieces of rabbit, pork, liver and bacon, turning them until browned.
3. FLAME WITH BRANDY: see p.68.
4. When the flames have died down, remove the liver and chop it into small pieces. Add this, with the rabbit, pork and bacon to the casserole.
5. Rinse the frying pan with a little stock and add this to the casserole.
6. Wash the mushrooms and add to the casserole.
7. Add the herbs and the wine and then top up with stock to cover.
8. Season with a little salt and freshly ground black pepper.
9. Put the casserole into the preheated oven and cook for 1¹/₂ hours.

TO THICKEN THE SAUCE

❏ Remove the casserole from the oven and ladle the liquid into a heavy based saucepan. Put onto a medium heat.
❏ Dissolve a heaped teaspoonful of potato flour in

¹/₂ a cup of cold water. Add carefully to the liquid, stirring briskly, until it has thickened to the consistency of gravy. Simmer for 2 to 3 minutes.

❑ Return the thickened sauce to the casserole.

THE CIVET WILL KEEP HOT WELL UNTIL READY TO SERVE.

—ooOoo—

FRENCH CASSEROLE OF LAMB WITH HERBS

A favourite with my daughters. "Can we have French lamb stew?" was the cry when they were young. "What makes it French?" you might ask. Well, just that the recipe originated from "Auntie" in Paris, where I first enjoyed it over 40 years ago.

Use a shoulder of lamb and ask your butcher to bone it for you. ALLOW 250gr (¹/₂lb) per person. Keep the bones for stock, and ALLOW ENOUGH TIME (¹/₂ to 1 hour) TO MAKE THE STOCK.

As the casserole has carrots in it, you can serve it with only plain boiled, creamed or new potatoes or you may like an additional green vegetable. Use one that is in season like cabbage, spring greens, broccoli or beans.

TO SERVE 4 TO 6 YOU WILL NEED:
1 Boned Shoulder of Lamb
2 Medium Onions
6 Medium Carrots
3 Sticks of Celery
Sprig Parsley
3 Sprigs of Thyme or 1 heaped tsp
2 Bay Leaves
600ml /1pint Stock
Unsalted Butter
Mild Olive Oil
Salt & Freshly Milled Black Pepper
Freshly Chopped Parsley

PREPARATION AND METHOD
Preheat your oven to 150ºC / Gas Mark 2.

❑ Cover the bones in cold water, bring to the boil and simmer for ¹/₂ to 1 hour, **with the lid off**, to make a stock.

1. Trim off as much fat, gristle and skin as you can from the lamb and cut into double bite-sized pieces.
2. Skin the onions and cut into small chunks.
3. Peel the carrots and slice.
4. Chop the celery into small pieces.
5. Heat a knob of butter and a little oil in a frying pan over a medium to high heat. When it is sizzling, fry the lamb pieces, turning until golden brown. Remove to a cast-iron casserole.
6. Fry and brown the vegetables and add to the casserole with the bay leaves, parsley and thyme.
7. Add enough stock to the casserole to cover the meat and vegetables and season with salt and freshly milled black pepper.
8. Place in the preheated oven and cook for 1¹/₂ to 2 hours.

Chicken and Ham Pie

Recipe p.164

Escalope of Pork Normande
Recipe p.140

TO THICKEN THE SAUCE
- ❏ Ladle the liquid from the casserole into a saucepan and bring to the boil.
- ❏ Dissolve a heaped teaspoonful of potato flour in $\frac{1}{2}$ a cup of cold water and slowly add to the boiling liquid, stirring briskly, until you have a good gravy consistency. Simmer for 2 to 3 minutes and return to the casserole.

SERVE from the casserole sprinkled with freshly chopped parsley.

NAVARIN OF LAMB

This traditional French dish has a very distinctive flavour and, with the vegetables and small new potatoes cooked in the casserole, is a complete meal, see illustration p.117.

Before the year-round availability of most vegetables, even new potatoes, navarin was essentially a casserole for the spring. You can however, if you have no new potatoes, cook potatoes separately and add them just before serving.

Ask the butcher to bone a shoulder of lamb and keep the bones to make a stock. ALLOW $\frac{1}{2}$ TO 1 HOUR TO MAKE A STOCK.

TO SERVE 4 TO 6 YOU WILL NEED:
1 Boned Shoulder of Lamb
3 Medium Carrots
2 Onions
2 Small Leeks
3 Sticks of Celery
4 Tomatoes
12 to 16 Small New Potatoes
Tomato Purée
Potato flour
1 to 2 Cloves of Garlic
2 Bay Leaves
1 Sprig Thyme or 1 tsp dried
90gr /3oz Caster Sugar
Unsalted Butter
Mild Olive Oil
Salt & Freshly Milled Black Pepper

PREPARATION AND METHOD
Preheat your oven to 150°C/Gas Mark 2.
Put the bones into a saucepan, cover in water and boil, **without a lid**, for $\frac{1}{2}$ to 1 hour to make stock.
1. Trim as much fat, gristle and skin from the lamb as possible and cut into double bite-sized pieces.
2. Cut a cross in the base of each tomato, place them in a bowl and cover with boiling water. After about 2 to 3 minutes, plunge them into cold water then remove the skins. Cut into small pieces.
3. Skin the onions and cut into small chunks.
4. Strip the outside leaves from the leeks, trim to leave approximately $\frac{2}{3}$ white and $\frac{1}{3}$ green. Wash them under cold running water, **holding them upside-down**, so as to wash any grit out and not further into the root. Cut into pieces about 2·5cm (1") long.
5. Wash the celery and chop into small pieces.
6. Scrub or peel the potatoes.
7. Skin the garlic, chop and crush.

8. Take a large frying pan and melt a knob of butter and a little oil over a high heat. When sizzling, add the pieces of lamb, season with a little salt and freshly milled black pepper and **when the pan has returned to full heat**, liberally sprinkle with caster sugar to caramelise, i.e. the sugar will go through a frothing stage and then become golden brown and, fairly quickly after, dark brown — just before burning! **Immediately douse with a ladle of stock**. Transfer to the casserole.

It is essential you wait for the sugar to caramelise, otherwise the dish will be too sweet and lack its distinctive flavour. But be careful to catch it before it burns .

9. In the same frying pan, add another knob of butter and lightly sauté the onions, carrot and garlic. Add to the casserole with all the other ingredients, including the new potatoes.
10. Cover the meat and vegetables with stock and stir in 2 teaspoons of tomato puree.
11. Cook, with a lid on, in the preheated oven, for $1^3/_4$ hours.

TO THICKEN THE SAUCE:
- ❏ Ladle the liquid from the casserole into a saucepan and bring to the boil.
- ❏ Dissolve a heaped teaspoon of potato flour in $^1/_2$ cup of cold water and slowly add to the boiling liquid, stirring briskly until you have a good gravy consistency. Simmer for 2 or 3 minutes and return to the casserole.

THE NAVARIN WILL NOT SPOIL IF KEPT HOT UNTIL READY TO SERVE.

SECRET OF SUCCESS: caramelising the sugar is crucial and gives the unique flavour which is the essence of this dish and makes it quite different to any other casserole.

—ooOoo—

BOEUF À LA BOURGUIGNONNE

In its classic form this wonderful French dish was made with sautéed steak, dressed with red wine sauce and a garnish of onions, mushrooms and salt pork. Absorbed into French country cooking and made as a casserole, there are many variations. My recipe is based on a superb version that I had in a country restaurant in Burgundy, the region from which it comes.

I use top rump, as it is tender and requires less cooking than chuck.

Flaming with brandy is used in this dish. See full instructions on p.68.

Boeuf Bourguignonne is a rich dish, so is best served with simple mashed, boiled or new potatoes to complement it. Carrots, beans or celery are all an excellent second vegetable.

TO SERVE 4 YOU WILL NEED:
750gr /1¹/₂lb Top Rump
1 Medium Onion

Smoked Salmon & Scrambled Egg

Recipe p.180

1 Clove of Garlic
Sprig of Thyme or 1/2 tsp dried
Sprig Parsley
1 Bay Leaf
1/3 Bottle of Red Burgundy
2 Tablespoons Brandy
300ml /1/2 pint Stock
Tomato Purée
Unsalted Butter
Mild Olive Oil
Potato Flour
Salt & Freshly Milled Black Pepper

For the Garnish:
125gr /4oz Green Streaky Bacon, **in the piece**
60gr /2oz Button Mushrooms
16 Baby Onions
Fresh Chopped Parsley

PREPARATION
Preheat your oven to 150°C/Gas Mark 2.
❏ Cut the steak into thick slices, to make two pieces per person.
❏ Skin and cut the onion into small cubes.
❏ Peel, chop, and crush the garlic.

METHOD
1. Place a large knob of butter and a little oil in a frying pan on a high heat. Fry the onion and garlic until slightly brown. Transfer to a cast-iron casserole.
2. Add a little more oil to the frying pan. When sizzling hot, put in the pieces of steak and brown them quickly on both sides.
3. TO FLAME: see p.68.
4. When the flames have died down, place the steak in the casserole. Rinse out the frying pan with a little stock, adding 2 teaspoons of tomato purée and add this to the casserole.
5. Add the wine and herbs to the casserole with enough extra stock to cover. Season with a little salt and freshly milled black pepper.
6. Place in the preheated oven with a lid on and cook for 1 1/2 hours.

WHILE YOUR CASSEROLE IS COOKING, YOU CAN PREPARE THE GARNISH
❏ Remove the skin and any gristle from the piece of bacon and cut into small cubes.
❏ Skin the onions. They should be of fairly uniform size so, if necessary, remove an extra layer or two from the larger ones.
❏ Wash the mushrooms and, leave whole or cut in half.

The garnish should be cooked as near to serving time as possible or it will spoil:-
1. Put a frying pan with a little oil over a medium heat. Fry the bacon pieces until golden. Remove and keep hot.
2. Add a little butter to the pan and add the onions, cook with a lid on until tender. Remove and keep hot.
3. Add more butter if needed and quickly fry the

mushrooms. Remove and keep hot.

WHEN THE CASSEROLE IS COOKED, THICKEN THE SAUCE:-

1. Remove the pieces of steak from the casserole and arrange on your serving dish. Cover and keep hot.
2. Mix a heaped teaspoon of potato flour with $1/2$ a cup of cold water and stir until dissolved. Add slowly to the boiling liquid, stirring briskly, until you have the consistency of gravy. Simmer for 2 to 3 minutes. Check the seasoning.

TO SERVE, dress the steak with the sauce, top with the garnish and sprinkle with fresh chopped parsley.

THE SECRET OF SUCCESS is in the garnish which, while enhancing the attractive presentation of this dish, also adds a wonderful contrast of flavours and texture.

CASSEROLE OF STEAK AND VENISON WITH GUINNESS AND PORT

Sometimes venison is sold too fresh. It is at its best when well hung. Don't be put off by the raw smell for, when cooked, the meat has a full, rich flavour.

Very good served with creamed potatoes, cabbage or carrots, which balance the rich flavours of the casserole.

ALLOW $1/2$ TO 1 HOUR TO MAKE THE STOCK IN ADVANCE.

TO SERVE 4 YOU WILL NEED:

500gr /1lb Chuck or Top Rump Steak
375gr /12oz Stewing Venison
2 Medium Onions
2 Teaspoons Tomato Purée
Unsalted Butter
Mild Olive Oil
Sprig of Parsley
2 Sprigs Thyme or 1 tsp dried
1 Bay Leaf
3 Cloves in Sachet (see p.23)
Small Can (or $1/2$ pint) Guinness or Stout
100ml /4fl.oz Port
300ml /$1/2$ pint Stock
Potato Flour
Salt & Freshly Milled Black Pepper
Freshly Chopped Parsley to Garnish

PREPARATION AND METHOD

Preheat your oven to 150°C/Gas Mark 2.

1. Trim any gristle and skin from the steak and venison and place these trimmings in a small saucepan with 600ml /1 pint water. Simmer for $1/2$ an hour to 1 hour to make a stock.
2. Cut the meat into bite-sized cubes.
3. Skin the onions and cut into cubes.
4. Heat a small knob of butter and a little oil in a frying pan until bubbling. Add the onion and cook until slightly brown. Transfer to a cast-iron casserole.
5. Add a little more butter to your frying pan and, when it is sizzling, fry the pieces of meat until

browned. Transfer to the casserole.

6. Sprinkle with thyme and add the parsley, bay leaf, sachet of cloves and tomato purée.
7. Add the Guinness or stout and top up with stock to cover. Season with salt and freshly milled black pepper.
8. Cover the casserole, place in the preheated oven and cook for 2 hours.

TO THICKEN THE SAUCE

1. Remove the casserole from the oven and ladle liquid into a saucepan, add the port and simmer for 10 minutes. Keep the casserole hot.
2. Mix 1 heaped teaspoon of potato flour with $\frac{1}{2}$ a cup of cold water and add carefully to the saucepan until the sauce is the consistency of thickened gravy. Simmer for 2 to 3 minutes, return to the casserole and blend in.

TO SERVE sprinkle with fresh chopped parsley.

—ooOoo—

BRAISED OXTAIL

When eating game one is, of course, on the lookout for shot, but imagine my surprise one day when, eating oxtail, I found lead shot embedded in the meat! Was it a 'gun' swinging in on a low bird or one who, having failed to find his mark all day, chose an easier target? I am pleased that I was not standing next in line, but it must have given the poor bullock one hell of a fright!

Braised oxtail is a wonderfully rich and gooey dish. The sauce probably has the best flavour of all beef dishes.

Serve braised oxtail with creamed potatoes and a green or root vegetable.

In your planning, ALLOW ENOUGH TIME TO SOAK THE HARICOT BEANS FOR 4 TO 6 HOURS OR OVERNIGHT.

TO SERVE 4 TO 6 YOU WILL NEED:

2 Oxtails
2 Medium Onions
6 Medium Carrots
3 Sticks of Celery
Fresh Beef Stock or ($\frac{1}{2}$ Chicken Stock Cube & Water)
Tomato Purée
Plain Flour
Unsalted Butter
Mild Olive Oil
125gr /4oz Dried Haricot Beans
2 Bay Leaves
Fresh Chopped Parsley
Salt & Freshly Milled Black Pepper

PREPARATION AND METHOD

Soak the haricot beans in cold water for 4 to 6 hours, or overnight.

Preheat your oven to 150C/Gas Mark 2.

Oxtails are usually cut into pieces by the butcher but, if you tackle a whole one, you will find dips and mounds along the vertebrae. **If you cut through the mounds with a sharp knife you will miss the bones**. Use the whole tail, including the thin pieces, for they add taste. **It is important to trim off most of the fat to prevent the dish being too greasy**.

1. Having cut the tail then trimmed the pieces, coat them with plain flour and season with salt and pepper.
2. Skin the onion and cut into small chunks.
3. Peel and slice the carrots.
4. Wash the celery and cut into small pieces.
5. In the absence of fresh stock, put $1/_2$ chicken stock cube in a bowl or jug and pour over 900ml /$1 1/_2$ pints of boiling water to make a stock.
6. Using a large frying pan, melt a little butter and oil over a medium to high heat. Brown the pieces of meat and remove a cast-iron casserole.
7. Fry the vegetables until browned and add to the casserole.
8. Drain the beans and add to the casserole.
9. Place an extra knob of butter in the frying pan with the juices, stir in a heaped tablespoon of flour and gradually ladle in the stock, stirring and mixing with a wooden spoon until you have the consistency of thin gravy. If necessary, remove the pan from the heat, to avoid getting lumps.
10. Add 1 tablespoon of tomato purée and blend in well.
11. Pour this sauce into the casserole, straining through a sieve if lumpy, to cover the contents. Add the bay leaves and put on the lid.
12. Place in the preheated oven and cook for 3 to $3 1/_2$ hours.
13. Remove from oven and stand for a few minutes to allow the fat to settle on top. Scoop off any surplus fat. Check the seasoning.

SERVE from the casserole, sprinkled with fresh chopped parsley.

—ooOoo—

PASTRY & PIES
the secret of successful shortcrust pastry and
savoury pies

THE SECRET OF SUCCESSFUL SHORTCRUST PASTRY

Many cooks feel that they cannot make pastry, believing they "Haven't the hands". I suppose the most frequent question I have been asked over the years is "How do you make such light pastry?". An American lady once asked "Did you make that crust?.... what, with your **hands**?". The Americans are the only people I know who invented machines before hands!

In this book I have limited pastry-making to shortcrust. It is important to vary shortcrust pastry according to its use and I make different ones for savoury pies, fruit pies and pastry bases for sweet flans and tarts. In this section I deal with the general secrets of all pastry making with recipes for savoury pies and savoury suet crust, recipes for sweet pastries are in the pudding section.

Some cooks are satisfied with machine made pastry but, if you want a first class result, there really is no substitute for your hands. However, you can forget all you have read about cool hands and cold marble slabs! Not only that, have your ingredients ready at **room temperature**!

There is no 'mystique' in pastry making. Have confidence and, if you follow the method I have been using for what seems like 100 years, you will have enthusiastic praise for your pies!

You can economise by keeping ends of pastry, wrapped in clingfilm in the fridge for 1 or 2 days, or in the deepfreeze for use later. Equally you can save time by making pastry in advance and keeping it ready for use in the same way.

THE IMPORTANT THINGS TO WATCH FOR AND WHICH MAKE THE DIFFERENCE BETWEEN SUCCESS AND FAILURE ARE :

Too much water will produce a hard or tough result. Too little water and you may have difficulty rolling the pastry out and topping your pie. But do not worry too much, the finished article will be very 'short' (crumbly) and delicious. **Pastry needs a dry oven**, so do not cook it at the same time as a roast, casserole or anything that may produce steam.

Always make sure that your oven has reached the correct temperature before baking your pies and **place the pies in the centre of the oven.** Finally, **never put the pastry on your pie until the ingredients are cold, otherwise the steam will toughen it.**

Sifting the flour and using a lifting action when blending the flour and fat, introduces air to the mix, an essential ingredient for light pastry.

I always plump for taste and texture, rather than good looks, so I do not bother too much about dressing up my pies with leaves etc., by the time they are cooked they look golden and delicious.

These are the **SECRETS OF SUCCESS** for pastry making! Good Luck!

SHORTCRUST PASTRY (FOR SAVOURY PIES)

If you read the introduction to this chapter, you will see that I tell you to forget most of the things you have previously been told about pastry making. My wife, when she saw me making pastry for the first time, said that I had broken every golden rule! Be that as it may, it works!

YOU CAN MAKE PASTRY IN ADVANCE AND KEEP IT IN THE FRIDGE, WRAPPED IN CLING FILM FOR A DAY OR TWO, OR DEEP FREEZE IT.

TO TOP A PIE FOR 4 YOU WILL NEED:

250gr /¹/₂lbPlain Flour
90gr /3oz Lard
*90gr /3oz **Hard** Margarine**
Pinch of Salt
Water

PREPARATION & METHOD
Preheat your oven to 200°C /Gas Mark 6.

Have your fat at room temperature. (This is contrary to most advice, but really is the answer). ***Use block, not soft table margarine.**

1. Sift the flour and salt into a large mixing bowl.
2. Cut the lard and margarine into small knobs and add to the flour.
3. Using your fingertips and thumbs and **keeping your hands palm uppermost**, work the fat into the flour, **lifting all the time**. Continue this process by lifting the ingredients and rubbing them between the open fingers of your hands until most of the mixture resembles breadcrumbs, but **leaving some pieces of fat in small lumps**, not fully rubbed in. This will give the pastry a more open texture. By lifting the mixture and letting it fall back into the bowl, you are introducing air — an essential ingredient. **Work quickly!**

4. Now, **this is where most failures in pastry making occur**, add the water. **Add only a little at a time.** You can always add a little more, but too much and the pastry is spoilt. With a criss-cross movement, using a carving fork or large blunt knife, work in the water until you have a firm consistency then, with a little sprinkle of flour, form it **quickly and gently** into a ball with your fingers.

5. **Let the pastry "rest" before rolling out** — ideally for about ¹/₂ an hour in the fridge. This is not essential, but you will find it makes the pastry easier to handle.

Having made your pie crust do not 'play' with it and spoil it. Speed in rolling out is most important, so try to roll the pastry only once, as lightly as possible. If your pastry tears as you top your pie, patch it together and do not try to roll it again. By the time it is baked this will not show.

Make sure that your ingredients are cold before putting the pie together, or the steam will toughen and spoil the pastry.

SECRET OF SUCCESS: stop worrying and make your pastry **quickly**, with gay abandon!

CHICKEN AND HAM PIE

This is a using-up dish, made with cooked meats and it can be varied by substituting cold turkey or guinea-fowl for the chicken. Use about ¾ chicken and ¼ ham, but the exact amount is not crucial.

Serve the pie hot with vegetables or cold with salad. It is especially good with a selection of French salads. Perfect, too, for a picnic. See illustration p.152.

TO SERVE 4 YOU WILL NEED:
500gr /1lb Shortcrust Pastry (p.163)
Approx. 375gr /³/₄ lb Cooked Chicken
Approx. 125gr /¹/₄lb Cooked Ham
30gr/1oz Plain Flour
30gr/1oz Unsalted Butter
1 Teaspoon Dried Thyme
1 Clove of Garlic
1 Small Onion
300ml /¹/₂ pint Chicken Stock or Stock made with ¹/₄ Chicken
*   Stock Cube*
1 Egg
Salt & Freshly Milled Black Pepper

PREPARATION
❏ On a board, chop the cooked meat together and place in a bowl.
❏ Skin and finely chop the onion (method on p.50).
❏ Skin and crush the garlic.

METHOD
1. Bring the stock to the boil in a saucepan.
2. Melt the butter in a small, heavy based saucepan, add the onion and garlic and cook until transparent, but **do not brown**. Add the dried thyme and flour. Stir to form a roux, which should look like fatty breadcrumbs. Cook for 2 to 3 minutes.
3. Removing from the heat for a moment, carefully add a dribble of stock with a ladle, return to the heat and stir vigorously. Repeat until the sauce has a texture of thick double cream. Set aside to cool.
4. In a bowl, add the sauce to the cooked meat, mix well together and season with salt and freshly ground pepper.

WHILE THE FILLING COOLS, MAKE YOUR PASTRY (see shortcrust for savoury pies p.163).

TO ASSEMBLE THE PIE
Preheat your oven to 200°C/Gas Mark 6.
1. Cut the pastry into two.
2. Paint a 10" plate with melted butter and dust with flour.
3. Quickly roll out half the pastry, on a floured surface, to fit the plate. **Speed in handling the pastry makes for lightness**. Line the plate and, with a sharp knife, trim off the surplus pastry.
4. Add the surplus pastry to the rest and roll out to make the top.
5. Arrange the **cold** filling on the pastry base. Wet the edges of the pastry and cover with the top, **taking care not to stretch the pastry**. Pinch the edges together and trim off any excess. Cut three slots in the top, to allow the steam to escape.

6. When ready to bake, **not before or the pastry will spoil**, brush with beaten egg and place in the **centre** of the preheated oven. Bake for 30 to 35 minutes.

—ooOoo—

GUINEA-FOWL, PORK AND MUSHROOM PIE

My second recipe from the brace of guinea-fowl (the first is on p.123) is a pie made from the legs which you will have put aside in the fridge or freezer. You can also use chicken or turkey legs. ALLOW ENOUGH TIME FOR THESE TO THAW.

This pie uses pickling spice. Spices have always played an important role in traditional English cookery and give this pie its essential flavour. THE PIE FILLING CAN BE MADE IN ADVANCE.

TO SERVE 4 YOU WILL NEED:
500gr /1lb Shortcrust Pie Pastry (p.163)
4 Legs of Guinea-fowl
1 Pork Fillet (approx. 375gr/12oz)
2 Medium Onions
250gr /8oz Button Mushrooms
Sprig of Parsley
Sprig of Thyme or ¹/₂ tsp dried
1 Bay Leaf
2 Tablespoons of Whole Pickling Spice
900ml /1¹/₂ pints Fresh Chicken Stock or Water with ¹/₂ Chicken Stock Cube
Potato Flour
1 Beaten Egg to Glaze

PREPARATION
❑ Cut the pork fillets into cubes.
❑ Peel the onion and cut into small chunks.
❑ Wash the mushroom and, if large, slice them thickly.
❑ Make a sachet of pickling spice (see p.23), discarding the red chilli pods, as they are too hot.

METHOD
1. Bring the stock to the boil in a cast-iron casserole, add the herbs, sachet of pickling spice, onion, pork and guinea-fowl legs. Put the lid on and simmer for 45 minutes.
2. Add the mushrooms and continue to simmer for a further 15 minutes.
3. Strain the liquid into a saucepan and put the meats etc., aside to cool.
4. Bring the strained liquid to the boil on a medium heat.
5. Mix a heaped teaspoon of potato flour with ¹/₂ a cup of cold water and add very gradually to the boiling liquid, stirring until it is the consistency of gravy. Be careful not to add too much. Set on one side to cool.

WHILE THE FILLING COOLS, MAKE YOUR PASTRY (see pastry for savoury pies p.163).

TO ASSEMBLE THE PIE
Preheat your oven to 200°C/Gas Mark 6.
1. When all the ingredients are cool, strip the guinea-fowl meat off the bones and cut into pieces.

Discard the skin, bones, gristle, spice sachet and herbs.

2. Place a pie funnel or inverted egg cup in the centre of a pie or ovenproof dish and put the guinea-fowl, pork and mushroom into it with enough of the thickened stock to moisten, keeping the remainder to serve with the pie.

3. Roll out the pastry, on a floured surface, allowing 2.5cm (1") overlap all round.

4. Wet the edges of the pie dish with water and cover the pie, **taking care not to stretch the pastry**. Press down firmly onto the edges, then trim off the excess pastry. Cut these pieces into strips, damp the edge of the pie and lay the strips around it, then mould the edges with your finger and thumb. Cut two slots in the top to allow steam to escape.

5. **Just before baking, (no sooner, or the pastry will spoil)**, thoroughly beat the egg and paint the top of the pie.

6. Place in **centre** of the preheated oven to bake for 30 to 35 minutes.

If the pie filling has been made in advance and kept in the fridge, allow an extra 5 minutes cooking time.

SECRET OF SUCCESS is the addition of pickling spice, which gives the pie its distinctive flavour and of course light pastry.

—ooOoo—

RABBIT PIE

Rabbit pie should really be made with pickled pork but, as this is increasingly difficult to find, I use fresh belly and a little bacon for flavouring. If you are using wild rabbits, beware of finding shot when eating the pie! ALLOW ENOUGH TIME TO SOAK THEM FOR 2 TO 3 HOURS.

THE STOCK AND PIE FILLING CAN BE MADE IN ADVANCE.

TO SERVE 6 TO 8 YOU WILL NEED:
500gr /1lb Shortcrust Pastry (p.163)
2 Wild Rabbits or 1 Tame Rabbit (approx. 1k/2lb in weight)
250gr /8oz Belly of Pork
2 Rashers of Bacon
2 Medium Onions
Sprig of Parsley
Sprig of Thyme or ¹/₂ tsp dried
2 Bay Leaves
900ml /1¹/₂ pints Stock
Potato Flour
1 Egg to Glaze
Salt & Freshly Milled Black Pepper

IN ADVANCE
If you are using **wild rabbits**, wash them thoroughly inside and out and **soak them for 2 to 3 hours**, in salted water. Rinse and dry them.

In a traditional pie, the meat is left on the bone, but these days very few are willing to cope with bones. If you prefer to remove the bones you can do so after the rabbit is cooked.

TO JOINT THE RABBITS:
- ❑ Remove the fore and hind legs by slicing through the joint and breaking them off.
- ❑ Cut the back into 4 pieces up to the ribs. **To avoid bone splinters, feel along the vertebrae and cut through the top of a mound**.
- ❑ Place the ribs and head in a saucepan, cover with water and boil for 45 minutes, without a lid, to make a stock.

PREPARATION & METHOD
1. Skin the belly of pork. The best way to remove the skin is to cut the belly into strips. Lay each strip on your board, skin side down. Cut a flap of skin and hold this. Then, pressing down with your knife and working it backwards and forwards, pull and cut the skin off in one piece. Remove any bone from each strip, trim and cut into bite sized pieces.
2. Skin and chop the onion into small chunks.
3. Remove the rind and cut the bacon into small pieces.

WHEN THE STOCK IS READY :
4. Place the rabbit , pork, bacon, onion and herbs in a large saucepan or cast-iron casserole and cover with stock. Season with salt and freshly ground black pepper. Cover with a lid and simmer for $1\frac{1}{2}$ hours.
5. Mix one heaped teaspoon of potato flour with $\frac{1}{2}$ a cup of cold water. Stirring briskly, add gradually to the stew, until you have the consistency of gravy. Set on one side to cool.

WHILE THE FILLING COOLS, MAKE THE PASTRY (see shortcrust pastry for savoury pies p.163).

TO ASSEMBLE THE PIE
Preheat your oven to 200°C/Gas Mark 6.
1. Separate the meat from the gravy and place in a pie or baking dish, with or without bones. Add a little gravy (**enough to half cover the meat**). Keep the remainder to serve with the pie.
2. Set a pie funnel (or inverted egg cup) in the centre of the dish. Check the seasoning.
3. Roll out the pastry, on a floured surface, to the size of the dish, plus 2.5cm (1") overlap all around.
4. Damp the edge of the pie dish with water and cover the pie, **taking care not to stretch the pastry.** Press down the edges and trim off the overlap with a sharp knife.
5. Cut this excess pastry into strips. Damp the edge of the pie and lay the strips around the edge. Pinch them together with your finger and thumb to make a pattern around the edge. Cut two slots in the top to allow steam to escape during cooking.
6. **Just before baking, (no sooner, or the pastry will spoil)** beat the egg thoroughly and, with a pastry brush, paint the pie crust.
7. Place in the **centre** of the preheated oven to bake for 30 to 35 minutes.

—ooOoo—

STEAK AND KIDNEY PIE

This traditional recipe is simple and straightforward. No extra flavours are needed, just the combination of steak, kidney and onion, browned and casseroled. This browning process produces a flavour quite different from that of a steak and kidney pudding.

Serve steak and kidney pie with creamed potatoes (to mop up all that delicious juice!) and a fresh green vegetable or carrots.

TO SERVE 4 YOU WILL NEED:

500gr /1lb Shortcrust Pastry (p.163)
750gr /1½lb Top Rump, Chuck or Shin
250gr /½lb Ox Kidney in a piece
1 Medium Onion
Water
45gr /1½oz Unsalted Butter
1 Tablespoon Mild Olive Oil
Potato Flour
Salt & Freshly Milled Black Pepper
1 Egg to Glaze

PREPARATION AND METHOD

Preheat your oven to 170°C/Gas Mark 3.

1. Trim all the gristle and fat from the steak and cut into bite-sized pieces.
2. Slice the kidney in half lengthways, exposing the white core. Trimming ox kidney, you will find it easier to cut the flesh away from the core, rather than removing the core from the body of the kidney. Cut the flesh into small pieces.
3. Place all the trimmings in a saucepan with 900ml /1½ pints water and ½ teaspoonful of salt. Simmer for ½ to 1 hour to make a stock.
4. Skin and cut the onion into small chunks.

WHEN THE STOCK IS READY

5. Heat the butter and oil in a frying pan until sizzling. Brown the steak, kidney and onion and season with salt and freshly milled black pepper.
6. Transfer the contents of the frying pan to a casserole and add the stock. Season with salt and black pepper. Put in the preheated oven to cook for 1½ hours.
7. Remove from the oven and ladle the stock into a saucepan and put on a medium heat to boil. Mix a heaped teaspoon of potato flour with ½ a cup of cold water. Gradually add this to the liquid, stirring briskly, until you have a good gravy consistency. Set on one side to cool.

WHILE THE FILLING COOLS, MAKE THE PASTRY: (see shortcrust pastry for savoury pies p.163).

TO ASSEMBLE THE PIE

Preheat the oven to 200°C/Gas Mark 6.

1. Put the **cold** meats into a pie or baking dish and set a pie funnel in the centre.
2. Pour enough gravy into the pie dish to half-cover the meat. Set the rest aside to serve with the pie.
3. Roll out the pastry on a floured surface, allowing 2.5cm (1") overlap all round the pie dish.
4. Wet the edges of the pie dish and funnel and cover

the pie, **taking care not to stretch the pastry.** Press down the edges firmly and trim off the surplus pastry with a sharp knife.

5. Cut the excess pastry into strips. Damp the edges of the pie and cover with strips. Pinch together with your finger and thumb to make a pattern. Cut 2 slots in the top.

6. **When you are ready to bake the pie, not before,** beat the egg thoroughly and paint the crust. Place in the **centre** of the preheated oven and bake for 30 to 35 minutes.

SECRET OF SUCCESS: in my opinion steak and kidney pie should be left simple, without herbs, spices or wine. The resultant flavour is the rich combination of steak and kidney — unmasked!

—ooOoo—

STEAK AND KIDNEY PUDDING

I remember, as a child, grating butcher's suet and dusting it with flour for my mother to use. I have only occasionally used fresh suet, but if you can obtain and prepare it, it has a superior flavour. However, packet suet is perfectly satisfactory.

The instructions on packets of prepared suet tell you simply to stir the flour and suet together. I disagree! To obtain a lovely, light crust the suet should be at **room temperature and rubbed into the flour with a lifting motion in the same way as fat for pastry.**

There are variations of method and ingredients for a steak and kidney pudding but, correctly done, it should be completely different from steak and kidney pie. The raw ingredients are traditionally cooked in the pudding. This requires a long cooking time of 4 to 5 hours and does not produce much gravy. Having cooked steak and kidney pudding commercially, I have evolved a method which reduces this time to 2 hours, but retains the authentic taste and texture.

Some recipes advocate frying the ingredients and some the addition of stout or wine, but the distinctive and delicious flavour of a traditional pudding is lost.

I don't advise buying ready cut steak and kidney, because this is rarely well prepared.

Allow enough time for the steak and kidney filling to become cold before putting into the pudding. It can be made the day before.

Use a 1150ml/2 pint pudding basin.

TO SERVE 4 YOU WILL NEED:
750gr /1¹/₂lb Chuck Steak
250gr /8oz Ox Kidney
1 Medium Onion
90gr /3oz Plain Flour
600ml /1 pint Water
15gr /¹/₂oz Melted Butter
Salt & Freshly Milled Black Pepper
For the Suet Crust:
375gr /12oz Self-Raising Flour
185gr /6oz Shredded Suet
Water
Salt & Freshly Milled Black Pepper

ADVANCE PREPARATION AND METHOD

1. Trim the steak, removing fat, gristle and coarse skin and put the trimmings into a saucepan.
2. Cut the steak into bite-sized cubes.
3. Slice the kidney in half lengthways, exposing the white core. Trimming ox kidney, you will find it easier to cut the flesh away from the core, rather than removing the core from the kidney.
4. Cut the flesh into small pieces and add to the steak.
5. Put the core into a saucepan with the steak trimmings, cover with water and simmer for $\frac{1}{2}$ an hour to an hour to make extra stock.
6. Skin and cut the onion into small cubes.
7. Place the steak and kidney in a bowl and season well with salt and freshly milled black pepper, add the plain flour and toss to coat the meat.
8. Put the floured meat in a saucepan with the onion and water, stir and **place the lid on firmly**. Simmer for $1\frac{1}{2}$ hours then set aside to cool. **The filling must be cold before you assemble the pudding.**

WHEN THE FILLING IS COLD MAKE THE CRUST

❏ Sieve the flour and salt into a mixing bowl and add the suet. **With a lifting action and using your fingers tips, rub the suet into the flour**. It does not matter if some of the suet is not fully rubbed in.
❏ Add cold water carefully, mixing with a blunt knife, until you have an elastic texture, **a little more moist than pastry**. Dust the mixture with flour and mould it quickly and gently into a ball.

TO ASSEMBLE THE PUDDING

Put a kettle of water on to boil.

1. Paint the inside of a pudding basin with melted butter and dust with flour.
2. Cut a quarter off the dough and set on one side for the lid. Roll out the remainder and line the basin.
3. Separate the **cold** steak and kidney from its gravy. Put the meat into the lined basin and add enough gravy to almost cover the meat, reserving the surplus gravy to serve with the pudding. Season with a little freshly milled black pepper.
4. Roll the remaining crust to form a lid. Wet the edges of the suet crust lining and cover with the lid. Pinch the sides and lid together to seal.
5. TO COVER THE PUDDING take a square of greaseproof paper large enough to cover the top of the basin, with a good overlap (10cm/4") all round. Fold a pleat 4cm (1½") in the centre, to allow the pudding room to rise. Paint with melted butter and cover the pudding, butter side down. Secure with string or a rubber band.
6. Place the pudding into a steamer, or you can use a saucepan. With the latter, stand the pudding basin on an inverted saucer to keep the pudding off direct heat. Fill the saucepan to a level half way up the side of the basin with boiling water. **Do not overfill.**
7. Cook for 2 hours, with the water simmering, checking from time to time and adding more if necessary. Serve with the extra gravy.

SECRET OF SUCCESS: rubbing the suet into the flour gives a much lighter crust.

EGGS, PANCAKES & LIGHT MEALS

methods & recipes

EGGS, PANCAKES AND LIGHT MEALS

In this section I have given a small selection of easy-to-prepare meals but, once you have mastered making omelettes, scrambled egg, pancakes, cheese sauce, there is an infinite combination of meats, fish and vegetables to go with or fill these.

The attractive colours of Chasseur practical oven - to-table porcelain make a perfect foil for these informal meals. These dishes are also dishwasher, microwave and freezer safe.

CAULIFLOWER CHEESE

A good light lunch or supper dish, cauliflower cheese is easy and quick to make.

TO SERVE 4 YOU WILL NEED:
1 large Cauliflower

For the sauce:
45gr /1¹/₂oz Unsalted Butter
45gr /1¹/₂oz Plain Flour
Approx. 450ml /³/₄ pint Cauliflower Water
A little Milk
A little Cream (Optional)
60gr /2oz Grated Parmesan or 90gr /3oz Grated Cheddar or
    Gruyere
To finish
30gr /1oz Extra Grated Cheese
Cayenne Pepper

PREPARATION AND METHOD
1. Wash the cauliflower, then cook, (see p.43). **Keep the cooking water**.
2. Turn on the grill
3. Make the sauce: see method for Bechamel Sauce on p.16 but using the cauliflower water and a little milk in place of milk.
4. Stir in the cheese and a little cream and cook gently until the cheese has melted.
5. Put the cauliflower into a serving dish, pour over the sauce, sprinkle with the extra grated cheese and a little cayenne pepper.
6. Brown lightly under the grill and serve.

—ooOoo—

SAVOURY PANCAKES

When I introduced savoury pancakes to my lunchtime menu they were a runaway success!

The first time I made the mix, using a bowl and wooden spoon, my young assistant chef looked on with disbelief! To prove a point, I suggested he make the next batch with the food processor. He was totally converted to the superior result of the bowl and spoon!

You will find it easiest to use clarified butter for frying the pancakes, as it will not burn. Mild olive oil is a passable substitute.

A thick, and therefore heavy , frying pan is best for making pancakes. I find cast iron the best. In a thin, light pan the pancakes will stick.

TO MAKE 6 TO 7 PANCAKES YOU WILL NEED:

125gr /4oz Plain Flour
1 Large Egg
300ml /¹/₂ pint Skimmed Milk
¹/₂ Tablespoon Olive Oil
Clarified Butter
Pinch of Salt
Choice of Filling (see p.174)
Freshly Chopped Parsley to Garnish

METHOD

1. Sift the flour and salt into a mixing bowl and make a dip in the centre.
2. Break the egg into the dip and, using **a wooden spoon,** stir to gradually incorporate the flour.
3. Slowly add the milk, a little at a time, still stirring. If you are careful you should have a mix with the consistency of single cream and no lumps!
4. Set the pancake mix on one side to 'rest' for about ¹/₂ an hour.

This 'rest' is important, so now is the time to make your filling. You can have fun making up your own fillings, but I give two of my favourites: Ham, Mushroom, Tomato and Cheese on p.174 and Ratatouille on p.174.

TO MAKE THE PANCAKES

Turn on the grill to heat.

1. Take the rested batter and whisk in the oil, then pass through a sieve.
2. Put the frying pan onto a medium/high heat. Paint with clarified butter and, when really hot, ladle in about 50ml /2fl.oz of batter, tilting the pan to spread it thinly and evenly over the surface. Cook for about 1 minute and, with a palette knife, turn and cook the other side. **The exact amount of batter used for each pancake will depend on the size of your pan**.
3. Repeat the process, adjusting the quantity of mix to achieve a thin pancake. You may well have to discard the first one!

Keep the pancakes warm, stacked on a plate, until you have made them all.

TO ASSEMBLE THE PANCAKES

- ❏ Paint the baking tray with clarified butter.
- ❏ Put a pancake on the baking tray, place a good tablespoonful or more of your chosen filling into the middle, fold the sides to the middle and sprinkle with cheese. (This will help seal the pancakes into neat parcels).
- ❏ Move the first pancake to one side and repeat until baking tray is full.
- ❏ Place the filled pancakes under the grill to brown.

SERVE sprinkled with freshly chopped parsley.

—ooOoo—

RATATOUILLE AND CHEESE FILLING FOR PANCAKES

See recipe (p.54) for ratatouille. Take enough to fill the pancakes.

Reheat the ratatouille and have this ready, together with approximately 15gr/¹/₂oz of grated cheddar cheese to seal each pancake.

—ooOoo—

HAM, MUSHROOM, TOMATO AND CHEESE FILLING FOR PANCAKES

The ham can be left out to make a vegetarian pancake.

TO FILL 6 PANCAKES YOU WILL NEED:

6 Slices of Ham
375gr /12 oz Mushrooms
4 Tomatoes
185 gr /6oz Grated Cheddar Cheese
45gr /1¹/₂oz Butter
100ml /4 fl.oz Double Cream
Salt & Freshly Milled Black Pepper

PREPARATION

- ❏ Cut a small cross in the base of each tomato, place in a bowl and cover with boiling water. Allow to stand for 2 to 3 minutes and then douse in cold water. Skin and chop up.
- ❏ Wash and slice the mushrooms.
- ❏ Cut the ham into small pieces.

METHOD

1. Melt the butter in a thick based saucepan, add the mushrooms and cook for 2 to 3 minutes.
2. Add the tomato, ham, cream and half the cheese and simmer, stirring, for 2 minutes. Keep hot.

The remaining cheese will be used to seal the pancakes when filled.

—ooOoo—

174

HAM FLORENTINE

The combination of ham, spinach and cheese is very tasty! This is a very quick and easy meal, especially if you have the spinach ready in reserve in the freezer. If not, ALLOW ENOUGH TIME TO COOK THE SPINACH IN ADVANCE.

TO SERVE 4 YOU WILL NEED:
600ml/1pt Mornay Sauce (p.17)
4 Portions of Cooked Spinach
or 1k /2lbs Unprepared Spinach
6 Slices of Cooked Ham
60gr /2oz Extra Grated Cheese for the topping

TO ASSEMBLE THE DISH
Turn on the grill to heat.
1. Make the Mornay Suace.
2. Warm a serving dish under the hot grill.
3. Make four flat beds of spinach in the dish and return to the grill to heat through.
4. Lay 1¹/₂ slices of ham per person on each mound of spinach and cover with the cheese sauce.
5. Sprinkle with the extra grated cheese and lightly sprinkle with cayenne pepper.
6. Place under the grill again, until golden brown.

—ooOoo—

EGGS FLORENTINE

A poached egg nestling on a bed of spinach and coated with cheese sauce, lightly browned under the grill!

Many cooks use the addition of vinegar to the poaching water, to hold the eggs together, but I have occasionally detected a slight taste of vinegar which, for me, spoils the dish. I prefer to use salt.

I do not use poaching moulds, either, as these produce the texture of a boiled egg which bears no resemblance to the real thing!

Select a pan deep enough to cover the poaching eggs in water, but shallow and wide enough to enable you to remove the eggs with a slotted spoon or slice.

Use only fresh eggs. If not fresh the whites will disperse when poached.

MAKE THE MORNAY SAUCE AND COOK THE SPINACH IN ADVANCE. YOU CAN ALSO COOK THE EGGS SEVERAL HOURS IN ADVANCE, IF YOU KEEP THEM IN COLD WATER.

TO SERVE 4 YOU WILL NEED:
600ml /1 pint Mornay Sauce (p.17)
4 Portions Pre-cooked Spinach or
*   1k /2lb Unprepared Spinach*
2 Eggs Per Person
60gr /2oz Extra Cheese for the topping

PREPARATION
❑ Have the spinach and the mornay sauce ready.
❑ Grate the cheese.

METHOD

Turn on the grill to heat and place a bowl of cold water near the stove.

1. Fill your poaching pan with well salted water, about 4cm (1½") deep, and bring to the boil.
2. Break each egg separately into a cup or small basin. Take the pan off the heat and, **when the water is still,** slide each egg into the pan. Return to a low heat to **gently simmer.**
3. With a perforated spoon or slice, lift each egg out **before the white has fully set around the yolk** and place carefully in the basin of cold water.

It is important to cool the eggs before assembling the dish, or they will continue cooking and spoil.

4. Warm your chosen dishes under the hot grill.
5. Divide the spinach to make a base in each dish and put under the hot grill for 2 minutes to warm.
6. Lift the lightly poached eggs from the bowl with a perforated spoon, allowing the water to drain off, and put them onto the spinach bases. Cover with the mornay sauce and sprinkle with grated cheese.
7. Replace under the grill to slightly brown.

SERVE QUICKLY or the yolks will set.

SECRET OF SUCCESS: to have the water simmering very gently and it must be still before gently placing the eggs in the pan.

—ooOoo—

LEEK AND BACON AU GRATIN

This simple supper or light lunch dish is quick and easy to make, CAN BE PREPARED IN ADVANCE, warmed through in the microwave and finished under the grill.

Smoked bacon will add more taste to the dish than green bacon.

TO SERVE 4 YOU WILL NEED:
4 Rashers of Smoked Bacon
4 Medium Sized Leeks
For the sauce
45gr /1½oz Unsalted Butter
45gr /1½oz Plain Flour
60gr /2oz Gruyere or Cheddar Cheese
150ml /¼ pint Milk
300ml /½ pint Leek Cooking Water
Salt
Cayenne Pepper

PREPARATION & METHOD

Turn on the grill to heat.

1. Wash the leeks, upside down under a running tap of cold water, trim off any tough outer leaves and brown root, keep enough green to form about ⅓ to ⅔ of white. Tie together in bundles of 2 or 3, and cut in half.
2. Place in a pan of fast boiling salted water, **without a lid,** for 3 or 4 minutes, until tender but firm. Remove with a slotted spoon and keep warm. **Retain the cooking water.**
3. Remove the bacon rinds and place the bacon under the grill to cook until crispy.

TO MAKE THE SAUCE:

❑ Melt the butter in a thick based saucepan over a medium heat.

❑ Add the flour and stir briskly with a wooden spoon. Continue to stir and cook for 1 to 2 minutes. **Do not brown.**

❑ Gradually add the leek water and milk, starting with a dribble, stirring briskly all the time, until the sauce has the texture of single cream.

❑ Allow to simmer gently for 2 to 3 minutes whilst you grate the cheese.

❑ Add $2/_3$ of the grated cheese to the sauce and blend in.

4. Cut the leeks into chunks and put into an ovenproof dish.

5. Cut the bacon into small pieces and mingle with the leeks.

6. Add the cheese sauce and top with the remaining grated cheese.

7. Lightly sprinkle with cayenne pepper and brown under a hot grill.

—ooOoo—

PLAIN OMELETTES

"That's not an omelette, it's scrambled egg!" exclaimed a new chef."Pay attention and observe" I replied. "for this is the professional way to make omelettes." Reluctantly, young Robert conceded that he was convinced when he tasted the result!

Making the perfect omelette need not involve the slow and tedious method usually recommended, it is produced speedily, in fact in just seconds! You may well fail to achieve perfection the first few times, but eggs are not expensive and, with practice, well — just wait for the praise!

First, a word about your pan. **Don't use a non-stick pan.** Use cast iron ,steel-lined copper, or carbon steel and keep it exclusively for making omelettes.

Now for the perfect omelette! It should be light in texture, with a soft and creamy centre and not browned on the outside.

Clarified butter will give the best result, and it will not burn, but mild olive oil is an acceptable substitute.

YOU WILL NEED:

2 to 3 Eggs Per Person
Clarified Butter (see p.26)
Salt & Freshly Ground Black Pepper
Fresh Chopped Parsley to Garnish

PREPARATION

❑ Break the eggs for each person in separate bowls and add salt and pepper to taste. Do not beat the eggs until your pan is ready.

❑ Have your plate (or plates) ready warmed.

METHOD

1. Put your omelette pan on a medium to high heat and brush with clarified butter.
2. When it is sizzling hot, lightly beat the eggs with a fork and pour into the pan, quickly stir with the fork and **at the same time shake the pan to and fro**. Still shaking the pan, draw the egg away from the sides towards the middle **with a slightly lifting action.**

   Keep shaking, stirring and lifting until the required creamy texture is achieved, then quickly fold the omelette over and, holding the pan at a slight angle, give it a sharp tap and allow the omelette to roll out onto a warm plate.

Sprinkle with chopped parsley and serve immediately — **do not keep hot.**

SECRET OF SUCCESS is speed and mastery of the lifting, shaking motion. Only lightly beat the eggs.

—ooOoo—

FILLED OMELETTES

Prawn, ham, cheese, mushrooms and tomatoes all make good fillings for omelettes.

Have your chosen filling cooked and kept warm.

Prawn, ham and grated cheese can be warmed under the grill or in the microwave. Mushrooms should be sliced and tomatoes skinned and chopped and then cooked in a little butter.

To make the omelette, follow the instructions for plain omelettes and add the filling before folding over.

—ooOoo—

OMELETTE AUX FINES HERBES

This omelette is made by adding finely chopped fresh herbs to the eggs before lightly beating. Traditionally these are parsley, chervil, tarragon and perhaps spring onion or chives, enough of them to make the omelette slightly green. But it may be difficult to get all these fresh when required, so don't worry too much. My own favourite is just parsley on its own. Although I often use dried herbs in other recipes, **only fresh herbs will give a good result for omelettes.**

—ooOoo—

179

SMOKED SALMON AND SCRAMBLED EGG

This makes a simple and quick "brunch", light lunch or supper dish when you feel like a treat! Serve with brown or French bread and butter and don't forget to chill the white wine!

TO SERVE 4 YOU WILL NEED:

375gr /12oz Smoked Salmon
6 Large Eggs
45gr /1¹/₂oz Unsalted Butter
60ml /2¹/₂fl. oz Milk
Salt & Freshly Ground Black Pepper

PREPARATION
❏ Arrange the smoked salmon on plates, ready for the scrambled egg.
❏ Break the eggs into a bowl and season with salt and pepper.

METHOD
1. Place the butter and milk in a heavy saucepan on a high heat.
2. Whisk the eggs and, as the boiling milk and butter rises, frothing, in the pan, pour in the beaten eggs and whisk briskly.
3. Now take a **wooden spoon** and continue with a lifting and folding motion, making sure the eggs do not catch and burn.
4. **Remove from the heat whilst still quite moist** as the egg will continue to cook. Continue stirring and divide quickly onto your four plates.

SERVE STRAIGHTAWAY. **The texture should be light and creamy-moist.**

SECRET OF SUCCESS: wait until the milk and butter are really frothing. Thereafter, speed is of the essence! Don't overcook!

—ooOoo—

180

Making an Omelette   *Recipe p.177*

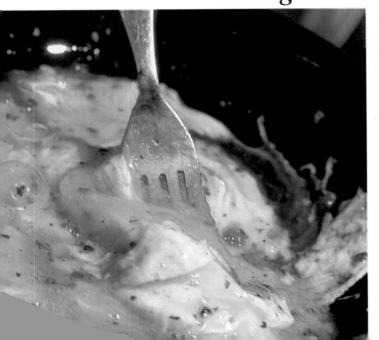

PUDDINGS
Methods and recipes

PUDDINGS

Puddings are not as widely made or used as they used to be but, when there is time and for special occasions, the old favourites are still the most popular.

For the purposes of this book, I have confined myself to well tried recipes from my own repertoire, some of which have been passed down two or three generations of my family and French flans and tarts from my late wife Jacqui's family. These incorporate the making of sweet shortcrust pastry, suet dough and sweet flan base pastry. Included, in addition, are a few favourites originating from my wife, Caroline whose criteria for adding any pudding to her repertoire is that it should not take any longer than 10 or 15 minutes to prepare! Others have kindly been passed on by friends, all of which we used with great success in our restaurant.

As well as pastry making, these recipes describe a number of techniques and skills, such as baking and steaming and making confectioner's custard, which can be applied to other recipes.

Before tackling pastry making in this section, may I refer you to the "Secret for successful shortcrust pastry" p.162. and to the preparation for the method for shortcrust pastry on p.163. The technique used is the same for all pastries in this book.

There, for the purposes of this book, I rest my case, since there are many books exclusively devoted to puddings and desserts for the more adventurous.

—ooOoo—

Making Pastry
Recipe p.162

Apple & Strawberry Crumble
Recipe p.193

TREACLE TART

With an empty plate a lady customer exclaimed "Well, there is only one way to describe that, it was orgasmic." This recipe for treacle tart has a lot to offer!

Use traditional bakers bread, not a wrapped loaf, and you will get a better taste and texture.

TO SERVE 4 YOU WILL NEED:
½ Small Loaf (approx. 8 slices)
435gr /14oz Golden Syrup
½ Lemon
30gr /1oz Unsalted Butter
For the Pastry:
185gr /6oz Plain Flour
125gr /4oz Unsalted Butter OR Block Margarine
1 Egg Yolk
Water
Pinch of Salt

TO MAKE THE PASTRY
Preheat your oven to 190°C/Gas Mark 5
1. Have the fat at room temperature.
2. Sift the flour and salt into a wide mixing bowl. Cut the butter or margarine into small pieces and add to the flour. **With a lifting action** to introduce air, blend the flour and the fat with your fingertips and thumbs until you have achieved a breadcrumb texture.
3. Separate the egg yolk, add 50ml /2fl.oz of cold water and whisk together. Then, carefully, **a little at a time,** add this to the pastry mix and, using a criss-cross action with a large fork or blunt knife, until you have a firm dough. **Better too dry than too wet.**
4. Dust your hands with flour and roll the dough quickly into a ball.

IT IS NOT ESSENTIAL, BUT YOU WILL FIND ROLLING OUT AND HANDLING EASIER IF YOU CHILL THE PASTRY, WRAPPED IN CLINGFILM, IN THE FRIDGE WHILST YOU PREPARE THE FILLING:

❑ Squeeze and keep the juice from ½ lemon.
❑ Cut the crusts off the bread and crumb it in a food processor (or with a grater)
❑ Warm the syrup and butter in a saucepan. Add to the breadcrumbs with the lemon juice and thoroughly mix together.

TO ASSEMBLE THE TART
1. Paint a removable base tart tin with a film of melted butter and dust with flour.
2. Roll out the pastry on a floured surface and line the tin, **taking care not to stretch the pastry.** Cut off the excess pastry.
3. Pour in the filling and bake in the preheated oven for 25 to 30 minutes.

I don't put a lattice on the top of my tart, but you can do so if you wish, with strips of pastry. This makes a more substantial tart.

BREAD AND BUTTER PUDDING

The essence of this old traditional and economical pudding is simplicity and the fact that, unlike many recipes, no eggs are used. I learnt it from my mother who, in turn, had learnt it from my grandmother, so it goes back over 100 years.

I remember my grandmother as a very capable, but awe-inspiring figure, straight backed and Victorian, dressed always in black bombazine with a velvet choker round her neck fastened with a diamond brooch, of whom my father would say: "That woman has no heart, she has a swinging brick." But no-one without a heart could make this perfect pudding!

Use baker's bread, rather than wrapped, to get the best taste and texture. Also use vanilla essence, not flavouring — they are quite different.

IF PREPARED IN ADVANCE, BREAD AND BUTTER PUDDING WILL REHEAT WELL IN THE MICROWAVE and with a Chasseur porcelain dish you can do this. It is usually served hot, but is also delicious cold, with a large dollop of thick cream! See illustration p.192.

TO SERVE 4 YOU WILL NEED:

12 Slices (day old) White Bread
125gr /4oz Softened Butter
750ml /1¼ pints Milk
185gr /6oz Sultanas
125gr /4oz Caster Sugar
2 Teaspoons Vanilla Essence
⅓ Whole Nutmeg (freshly grated)

METHOD

Preheat the oven to 200°C/Gas Mark 6.

1. Heat the milk and vanilla essence in the saucepan.
2. Remove the crusts from the bread and spread generously with butter
3. Place a layer of buttered bread in an ovenproof baking dish (not over-lapping).
4. Dredge liberally with sugar, then grate nutmeg directly all over the pudding and sprinkle with ⅓ the sultanas.
5. Repeat the process twice to form three layers.
6. Pour over the hot milk and vanilla and press down to soak up the milk. If necessary add a little more cold milk so that there is a slight excess. Finish with a final sprinkling of caster sugar. Allow to stand for 15 minutes before placing in the oven.
7. Cook for 30 to 35 minutes in the preheated oven and serve hot.

SECRET OF SUCCESS: is to achieve a subtle taste of nutmeg and vanilla, combined with just the right degree of sweetness.

—ooOoo—

Lemon Cheesecake
Recipe p.199

French Raspberry Tart
Recipe p.196

SPOTTED DICK

This is another old and traditional recipe nostalgically remembered by several generations as a "real" pudding.

Serve Spotted Dick with custard (see p.195) or, if you just don't care, eat it as they do in Lincolnshire, with a knob of soft butter and sprinkling of caster sugar!

Slices of Spotted Dick will reheat very well in the microwave, or you can fry slices in butter and sprinkle them with caster sugar, as my mother did before the advent of microwaves (or low cholesterol diets) and we all survived!

Traditionally steamed puddings were cooked in a cloth rather than a basin. If you prefer to make your pudding in this really simple and traditional way, use a cloth kept for the purpose. A 60cm (24 inch) square of plain white cotton is perfect. Flour the cloth and place the dough in the middle, gather the material together and tie with string, **allowing room for the pudding's volume to expand by about a quarter,** then place in a large pot of boiling water. It is particularly important not to allow the pot to go off the boil, or you will get a soggy result. Use a kettle of **boiling** water to top up when necessary. The cooking time is the same as when using a basin.

TO SERVE 6 TO 8 YOU WILL NEED:

375gr /12oz Self-Raising Flour
185gr /6oz Shredded Suet
125gr /4oz Currants
30gr /1oz Caster Sugar
30gr /1oz Butter
Water
Pinch of Salt

PREPARATION AND METHOD

1. Put a steamer, or large saucepan filled with enough water to come halfway up the side of a pudding basin, on a medium heat. If using a saucepan, put an inverted saucer into the bottom to keep the pudding away from direct heat.
2. Melt the butter and paint the inside of the pudding basin, then dust it with flour. Choose a basin that will hold 1150ml/2 pints of liquid.
3. Take a square of greaseproof paper large enough to cover the top of the basin, with a good overlap (10cm/4 inches) all round. Paint with melted butter, then fold a pleat 5 cm (2 inches) in the centre, to allow the pudding room to rise.
4. Weigh and sieve the flour and salt into a large mixing bowl and add the suet **(which should be at room temperature).**
5. Using your finger tips and a lifting action, work the suet into the flour, producing a light breadcrumbs consistency.

190

I KNOW SUET PACKETS TELL YOU TO JUST STIR IN THE SUET, BUT YOU WILL ACHIEVE A MUCH LIGHTER PUDDING IF YOU TAKE THE TROUBLE TO BLEND IT IN WITH YOUR FINGERS.

6. Add the sugar and currants and mix in well with your hands.
7. Add **cold** water, a little at a time, using a criss-cross action with a blunt knife, until you have a moist dough.
8. Sprinkle the dough with flour, roll it into a ball and place in the buttered basin.
9. Cover the pudding with the greaseproof paper, butter side down. Secure with string or a rubber band.
10. Put into the steamer or saucepan and steam over a medium heat for 2½ hours, checking the water level from time to time.

—ooOoo—

APPLE AND SULTANA CRUMBLE

Crumble topping can be used to make a variety of puddings. Apple and sultana is a favourite and in the summer apple and strawberry is delicious. Use plums, rhubarb or gooseberries when they are in season.

The secret is a light, rich butter crumble mix.

THE APPLE (OR OTHER FRUIT) CAN BE PREPARED IN ADVANCE. HAVE THE BUTTER AT ROOM TEMPERATURE.

TO SERVE 4 YOU WILL NEED:
750gr /1½lb Cooking Apples
90gr /3oz Sultanas
60gr /2oz Brown Sugar
½ Teaspoon Ground Cinnamon

For the Crumble Topping:
250gr /8oz Plain Flour
186gr /6oz Unsalted Butter
45gr /1½oz Caster Sugar
Pinch of Salt

PREPARATION & METHOD
1. Peel, core and cut the apples into quarters. Place in a saucepan of cold water, cover with a lid and bring to the boil. Keep an eye on it and **as soon as it boils** just turn the apple with a spoon to make sure it has all softened a little.
2. Strain off the water through a colander or sieve and put the apple into an ovenproof baking dish, mashing it down roughly with a wooden spoon.
3. Scatter on the sultanas and sprinkle with the brown sugar and a dusting of cinnamon. **Set on one side to cool.**

WHILE THE APPLE IS COOLING, MAKE THE TOPPING
Preheat the oven to 200°C/Gas Mark 6.
❑ Sift the flour and salt into a large mixing bowl.
❑ Cut the butter into small pieces and add to the flour.

Bread & Butter Pudding
Recipe p.187

❏ With the tips of your fingers rub and blend the butter into the flour, using a light lifting action to introduce air to the mixture. Add half the caster sugar and mix in.

TO ASSEMBLE THE CRUMBLE

1. **When the apple is cold**, cover it evenly with the crumble mixture and press down lightly around the edges. Sprinkle with the remaining caster sugar and pierce with a large fork about six times — this will allow the steam to escape.
2. Place in the preheated oven for 25 to 30 minutes, until it is a light golden brown.

SERVE hot or cold with custard (see p.195) or cream.

—ooOoo—

APPLE & STRAWBERRY CRUMBLE

See illustration p185.
Make as for apple and sultana crumble, replacing the sultanas, cinnamon and brown sugar with caster sugar and a punnet of strawberries cut into halves or quarters, to the apple when it is cool, before adding the topping. **It is important that the apple is cool before topping with the crumble mix.**

——ooOoo—

193

ENGLISH APPLE PIE

This is a traditional "plate" pie with pastry top and bottom. It relies on the wonderful flavour of Bramley apples. I prefer to make my apple pie without cloves.

This method of apple preparation produces a light and almost fluffy texture and the pastry is different from that used for savoury crusts. It is a pie that has always scored top marks!

TO SERVE 6 YOU WILL NEED:
750gr /1¹/₂lb Bramley Apples
60gr /2oz Caster Sugar
A Little Melted Butter
<u>For the Pastry:</u>
250gr /8oz cups Self-Raising Flour
*125gr /4oz Butter or **Block** Margarine*
Caster Sugar
Water
Pinch of Salt

PREPARATION AND METHOD
Preheat the oven to 200°C/Gas Mark 6
1. Peel, core and cut the apples into quarters.
2. Place them in a saucepan of cold water, cover with a lid and bring to the boil. Turn the apple in the boiling water until slightly soft. **Don't overcook**.
3. Strain through a colander or sieve. Chop roughly and set aside to cool.

TO MAKE THE PASTRY
1. Have the butter or margarine at room temperature.
2. Sift the flour and salt into a wide mixing bowl. Cut the fat into small pieces and add to the flour. **With a lifting action**, blend the flour and the fat with your fingertips and thumbs, keeping your hands palm uppermost. **Lifting all the time will introduce air into the mixture.** Work quickly until you have achieved a breadcrumb texture. Add 2 teaspoons of caster sugar and mix in.
3. **A little at a time,** add cold water and mix in using a criss-cross action with a carving fork or large blunt knife until you have a firm **but not wet** dough.
4. Blend the dough quickly and gently with your fingertips into a ball, using a sprinkling of flour. Put on one side to rest.

TO MAKE THE PIE
Melt a little butter and lightly paint the plate. Dust with flour.
1. Cut the dough into half and roll out the base on a floured surface. Put this onto the plate and trim off the edges.
2. Place the cold apple in the centre and add the sugar. Damp the edges of the pastry with water.
3. Roll out the top and cover the pie. Pinch the edges together and trim off the surplus pastry. Make three cuts in the top to let out the steam.
4. Bake in the preheated oven for 30 to 35 minutes.
5. Remove from the oven and, **whilst still hot**, sprinkle with caster sugar.

SERVE hot or cold with cream or custard sauce (see p.195).

CUSTARD SAUCE

Home-made custard is entirely different from that made with powder. It is simple to make, but don't try to hurry the process, take your time. The risk is that the mixture will curdle if it is allowed to boil, **so keep the heat low and stir continuously.**

Vanilla essence is infinitely superior to vanilla flavouring, so it is worth using this.

A heavy based saucepan is essential for making this custard, ideally Chasseur or copper, or you can use a double saucepan or bowl set over boiling water.

TO SERVE 4 YOU WILL NEED:
300ml /¹/₂ pint Milk
3 Egg Yolks
30gr /1oz Caster Sugar
1 Teaspoon Vanilla Essence
A Little Double Cream (optional)

PREPARATION & METHOD
1. Heat the milk and vanilla essence to boiling point.
2. Separate the yolks from the whites of the eggs, discarding the whites.
3. Thoroughly mix the egg yolks and sugar together in a bowl.

If you like a thick custard, you can cheat and add 1 teaspoon of cornflour to the eggs and sugar mix. This will also avoid any tendency for the custard to curdle.

4. Add the hot milk and whisk together. Return to the saucepan through a sieve.
5. Place the saucepan over a low to medium heat and stir constantly with a wooden spoon. **Do not allow to boil.** Continue cooking and stirring until the sauce thickens enough to coat the back of the wooden spoon.
6. To finish, you can add a little cream and stir in.

TO SERVE either keep hot in a bain marie or bowl over **just simmering** water, or allow to cool and chill.

—ooOoo—

FRENCH STRAWBERRY FLAN (TARTE AUX FRAISES)

These delicious fruit tarts can be found in almost every Patisserie in France. They consist of a crisp pastry base, a layer of confectioner's custard and fresh strawberries, topped with an apricot glaze. Other fruit can be used. Raspberries are particularly good, or peaches or grapes. Illustration p.189.

This recipe involves blind baking for which it is well worth having ceramic baking beans, but if you don't have any, substitute dried peas or beans.

THE PASTRY BASE AND THE CUSTARD CAN BE MADE UP TO A DAY IN ADVANCE. IF POSSIBLE ALLOW ENOUGH TIME FOR THE PASTRY TO 'REST' IN THE FRIDGE FOR $\frac{1}{2}$ TO 1 HOUR BEFORE ROLLING OUT, AS THIS WILL MAKE IT EASIER TO ROLL.

TO SERVE 6 YOU WILL NEED:

For the Pastry base:
185gr /6oz Plain Flour
125gr /4oz Unsalted Butter
30gr /1oz Caster Sugar
1 Egg Yolk
Approx. 50ml /2fl.oz Cold Water
Pinch of Salt

For the Custard:
3 Egg Yolks
80gr /2$\frac{1}{2}$oz Caster Sugar
15gr /$\frac{1}{2}$ oz Unsalted Butter
30gr /1oz Plain Flour
250 ml /9fl.oz Milk
1 Teaspoon Vanilla Essence

For the Glaze:
185gr /6oz Apricot Jam
Juice from $\frac{1}{2}$ lemon
50ml /2fl.oz Water

For the Filling:
375gr /12oz Fresh Strawberries

TO MAKE THE PASTRY BASE
Preheat the oven to 200°C/Gas Mark 6.
Have your butter at room temperature.

1. Sift the flour and salt into a mixing bowl.
2. Cut the butter into small knobs and add to the flour.
3. Using your fingertips and thumbs work the butter into the flour, **lifting all the time**. Continue this process by lifting the ingredients and rubbing them between the open fingers of your hands to introduce air until the mixture resembles breadcrumbs.
4. Add the sugar to the dry ingredients and mix well.
5. Mix the egg yolk and water together and add gradually to the dry ingredients, using a blunt knife or fork and a criss-cross movement, until you

have a firm consistency.

6. Now, with a little sprinkle of flour, form the pastry **quickly and gently** into a ball with your fingers.
· 7. Butter a removable base tart tin and dust with flour.
8. Roll the pastry out on a floured surface and, being careful not to stretch it, line the tin.
9. Cut the surplus pastry off by rolling the pin across the top of the tin, then prick all over the base with a fork.
10. Cover with a sheet of greaseproof paper and fill with the baking beans.
11. Place in the preheated oven and bake for 20 to 25 minutes.
12. Remove the beans and greaseproof paper and set on one side to cool.

TO MAKE THE CUSTARD (crème pàtissière)
Use vanilla essence, not flavouring, to get the best result.
1. Separate the egg yolks and set on one side.
2. Soften the butter.
3. Sift the flour through a sieve.
4. Bring the milk and vanilla to the boil in a saucepan.
5. In a small mixing bowl, thoroughly mix the soft butter and sugar together with a wooden spoon. Blend in the egg yolks and gradually add the sifted flour. Stir to form a smooth paste.
6. Using a whisk, gradually add and mix in the hot milk, stirring all the time.
7. Return to the saucepan and simmer and stir for 2-3 minutes.

8. Pour into a bowl and set aside to cool, stirring from time to time to avoid a skin forming.

WHEN COLD, FILL THE PASTRY BASE WITH THE CUSTARD, ABOUT 1CM THICK. ARRANGE THE STRAWBERRIES ON TOP, CUTTING THEM IN HALF IF VERY LARGE.

TO MAKE THE GLAZE
1. Place the jam, lemon juice and water in a thick based saucepan and bring to the boil.
2. Transfer to a basin and pass through a sieve back into the saucepan. Push the mixture through with a wooden spoon and scrape off any that gathers on the underside of the sieve.
3. Continue to boil for about 5 to 10 minutes, stirring from time to time, until, when you test a drop of the syrup on a cold plate, it sets.

FINISH THE FLAN by spooning the glaze over the fruit and spreading it with a pastry brush. Set aside to chill

SERVE on its own — no need for cream.

—ooOoo—

FRENCH APPLE TART (TARTE AUX POMMES)

The French seldom eat cream with tarts and I recommend you try this one without and appreciate the crisp fresh flavour.

TO SERVE 6 YOU WILL NEED:

185gr /6oz Pastry as for French Strawberry Tart.

For the filling:

4 Eating Apples (Golden Delicious are perfect)
60gr /2oz Sugar

For the Glaze:

185gr /6oz Apricot Jam
Juice from ¹/₂ Lemon
50ml /2fl.oz Water

PREPARATION AND METHOD

Preheat your oven to 200°C/Gas Mark 6.

1. Butter a removable base tart tin and dust with flour.
2. Roll out the pastry on a floured surface and line the tin, being careful not to stretch the pastry.
3. Cut off the surplus pastry by running a rolling pin across the top of the tin.
4. Cover with a sheet of greaseproof paper and fill with baking beans.
5. Place in the preheated oven and **part bake** for 10 minutes.
6. Take from the oven and remove the baking beans and greaseproof paper.

WHILE THE PASTRY IS BAKING, PREPARE THE FILLING

1. Cut the apples into quarters and remove the core, peel and slice thinly.
2. Arrange the sliced apples in the part baked pastry shell, starting in the middle and overlapping in circles until you reach the edge.
3. Dissolve the sugar with a little water (about two tablespoons) in a small saucepan, and boil to form a syrup.
4. Paint the edges of the apple slices with the syrup, using a pastry brush. **The sugar will caramelise during cooking and add colour and flavour.**
5. Place in the preheated oven and bake for 25 minutes.

TO MAKE THE GLAZE

1. Place the jam, lemon juice and water in a thick based saucepan and bring to the boil.
2. Transfer to a basin and pass through a sieve back into the saucepan. Push the mixture through with a wooden spoon and scrape off any that gathers on the underside of the sieve.
3. Continue to boil for about 5 to 10 minutes, stirring from time to time, until, when you test a drop of the syrup on a cold plate, it sets.

WHEN THE TART IS COLD, using a spoon and a pastry brush, cover the apple with hot glaze and set on one side to cool before serving.

—ooOoo—

CHOCOLATE MOUSSE

This is a real chocolate mousse, rich but not too heavy. The recipe was given to my wife by a friend who was renowned for her wonderful puddings. It has remained a family favourite ever since, not least because it is so quick and easy!

TO SERVE 4 YOU WILL NEED:

250gr /8oz Bar of Plain, Dark Chocolate
3 Eggs
2 x 179gr Tins Cream

PREPARATION AND METHOD

1. Using a bain-marie or a bowl over a pan of simmering water and break the chocolate into it. Cover and leave until the chocolate is soft. Remove the bowl and set on one side to cool slightly.
2. Separate the egg yolks from the whites, being careful **that not even a small amount of yolk gets into the whites.**
3. Beat the egg whites until they nearly stand in peaks. Not as stiff as for meringues.
4. Stir the egg yolks into the melted chocolate and add the tinned cream. Mix together.
5. Carefully pour, a little at a time, the chocolate and egg mixture into the egg whites, **folding them together without beating.** It does not matter if a few pieces of egg whites do not blend in.
6. Transfer to a serving bowl or individual pots. Chill in the refrigerator.
MAKE THE MOUSSE SEVERAL HOURS BEFORE SERVING.

LEMON CHEESECAKE

There are numerous recipes for cheesecake, many of which rely on gelatine for setting, which makes for a rather dull and heavy texture. This one is really light, tangy and extremely easy to make.

YOU CAN SUCCESSFULLY FREEZE THIS CHEESECAKE. YOU CAN ALSO MAKE IT THE DAY BEFORE REQUIRED.

TO SERVE 8 YOU WILL NEED:

400gr /12 oz Philadelphia Cheese
400 gr /12 oz Tin Sweetened Condensed Milk
3 lemons
$1/_2$ Teaspoon Vanilla Essence (not flavouring)

For the Base:
200gr /7oz Digestive Biscuits
125gr /4oz Unsalted Butter

PREPARATION & METHOD

1. Put the biscuits, a few at a time, in a food processor and reduce to coarse crumbs, leaving a few small bits OR put in a bowl and crush with the end of a rolling pin. **The second method is best, as the base is lighter and more crunchy if the biscuits are not too finely crushed.**
2. Cut the butter into pieces and melt in a saucepan over a medium heat. Add the biscuit crumbs and stir with a wooden spoon until they are well coated.
3. Tip the crumbs into a loose-base or springform tin

approximately 6cm (2½") x deep 20cm (8"). Press down with your fingers to form a base. Set to one side.

4. Squeeze the lemons and set the juice to one side.
5. Put the Philadelphia cheese, condensed milk and vanilla essence in the bowl a food mixer or use a hand whisk and beat until it begins to thicken (about 3 minutes).
6. Turn the mixer speed down and gradually add the lemon juice. When all the juice is incorporated, turn the mixer speed up again and finish beating for about 1 minute, or until the mixture is thick. Do not overbeat.
7. With a spatula, transfer the mixture to top the base. Shake the tin to settle the pudding, rather than smoothing the top.

ALLOW AT LEAST TWO HOURS FOR THE CHEESECAKE TO CHILL IN THE FRIDGE AND SET BEFORE SERVING.

—ooOoo—

RASPBERRY FOOL

A simple pudding — easy to make, delicious to eat! You can use fresh or frozen raspberries and the brandy or calvados makes it extra special.

TO SERVE 4 YOU WILL NEED:
250 gr /½ lb Raspberries
185 gr /6oz Icing Sugar
300 ml /½ pint Double Cream
50ml /2fl.oz Brandy OR better still, Calvados

PREPARATION & METHOD
1. Spin the raspberries in a food processor and strain through a sieve, using a wooden spoon, to remove the seeds.
2. Return the strained pulp to the processor and blend in the sifted icing sugar and brandy or calvados.
3. Beat the double cream, in a bowl, until it is stiff enough to form peaks.
4. Add the fruit mixture to the cream in the bowl, whisking it well together until blended.
5. Transfer to a serving bowl or individual mousse pots, ramekins or glasses. Chill in the fridge for 3 to 4 hours.

BEST SERVED THE SAME OR THE NEXT DAY, WITH SWEET, CRISP BISCUITS.

FRESH FRUIT TRIFLE WITH GRAND MARNIER

This is a "grown-up" trifle! No jelly and real confectioner's custard make all the difference from those childhood party pieces scattered with brightly coloured hundreds and thousands!

To my palate, sherry in trifle produces rather an varnishy aftertaste, hence the Grand Marnier which, because of its orange base, blends with the fruit. If you don't acquire an extravagant taste for it, Grand Marnier, like all liqueurs, keeps for months.

The addition of apple adds texture and "bite" and if you also have pineapple or peach available they are a nice addition. Use home-made sponge cake, if you can, or a packet of sponge cakes is nearly as good.

TO SERVE 4 YOU WILL NEED:
300ml /¹/₂ pint Confectioner's Custard (p.196/197)
Sponge Cakes
Raspberry Jam
1 x 500gr /1lb Punnet Raspberries
2 Apples
2 Slices Pineapple OR 1 to 2 Peaches (optional)
¹/₂ Lemon
50ml /2fl.oz Grand Marnier
1 Tablespoon Sugar
50ml /2fl.oz Water
150ml /5fl. oz Double or Whipping Cream

PREPARATION & METHOD
1. Choose a suitable dish. Split and spread the sponge with jam. Cut into pieces and lay in the dish to cover the bottom.
2. Peel, core and dice the apple finely.
3. Peel and cut the pineapple or peach into small dice, if you have them.
4. Squeeze the ¹/₂ lemon and set the juice on one side.
5. Spread the raspberries, apple and other fruit over the sponge.
6. In a saucepan, over a medium heat, dissolve the sugar in the water, then add the lemon juice and Grand Marnier. Mix together and pour evenly over the fruit and sponge. Press down lightly.
7. Cover with the confectioner's custard and put it in the fridge to chill.

TO SERVE cover the top with whipped cream smoothed down with a fork.

—ooOoo—

201

SUMMER PUDDING

The important ingredient in this deliciously refreshing pudding is the bread. Ready-sliced, wrapped bread has a rather slimy texture when soaked in the fruit juices, so I recommend that you use traditionally baked bread. Have it medium sliced at the bakers, or cut it yourself to this thickness.

The combination of fruits you use will depend on availability, but it is important to include black currants. The most interesting summer puddings are those with a mixture of fruits in which the berries explode with a wonderful tart contrast.

While the summer fruits are in season, put some red and black currants, which are more scarce, into the deep freeze and bring these out to mix with strawberries and raspberries which have a longer season. The pudding can also be made with all frozen fruits.

YOU CAN FREEZE THE WHOLE PUDDING WHEN IT HAS BEEN MADE WITH FRESH FRUITS.

TO SERVE 6 YOU WILL NEED:

1K /2lbs Mixed Soft Fruits
Ideally 250gr /¹⁄₄lb each of:
*   Raspberries*
*   Strawberries*
*   Blackcurrants*
*   Redcurrants*
125gr /4oz Sugar
100ml /4fl.oz Water

PREPARATION & METHOD

1. Wash the fruit, string the currants and hull the strawberries.
2. Place all the fruit in a saucepan with the sugar and water. Bring to the boil and stir gently with a wooden spoon for 1 minute.
3. Allow the fruit to cool and then, using a sieve, strain off the juice into a bowl.
4. Slice the bread and remove the crusts. Cut the slices so that they will fit into a 1150ml/2 pint pudding basin, slightly overlapping each other. Dip each piece into the fruit juice before lining the basin and press them gently into place.
5. Fill the mould with fruit, add a little juice and cover with more bread dipped in juice.
6. Place a weighted saucer or plate on top of the pudding to compress it and put in the fridge to chill, retaining the extra juice.

Loosen the pudding with a knife or spatula and then place upside down on a serving plate and shake to remove it from the basin.

TO SERVE: Set a slice of pudding in the centre of each plate and pour some of the extra juice around it. Serve whipped cream separately.

—ooOoo—

Acknowledgements

To my late wife Jacqueline and Aunt Louise,
who taught me the arts of cooking and appreciating good food.
To my wife Caroline,
without whose encouragement, energy and bullying
this book would never have appeared.
To my family and friends
for their wonderful help and enthusiastic support.

Ian Lye, Watlington, 1999.

For information about any product recommended in this book, and for your local stockist, contact

Dexam International Ltd.
Tel : 01428 647639
Fax : 01428 656476
e-Mail : housewares@dexam.co.uk